Workshop on Processing Historical Language 2017

Held in conjunction with NoDaLiDa 2017

NEALT Proceedings Series Volume 32

Gothenburg, Sweden
22 May 2017

Editors:

Gerlof Bouma
Yvonne Adesam

ISBN: 978-1-5108-4336-3

Printed from e-media with permission by:

Curran Associates, Inc.
57 Morehouse Lane
Red Hook, NY 12571

Some format issues inherent in the e-media version may also appear in this print version.

Printed by Curran Associates, Inc. (2017)

For permission requests, please contact the Association for Computational Linguistics at the address below.

Association for Computational Linguistics
209 N. Eighth Street
Stroudsburg, Pennsylvania 18360

Phone: 1-570-476-8006
Fax: 1-570-476-0860

acl@aclweb.org

Additional copies of this publication are available from:

Curran Associates, Inc.
57 Morehouse Lane
Red Hook, NY 12571 USA
Phone: 845-758-0400
Fax: 845-758-2633
Email: curran@proceedings.com
Web: www.proceedings.com

Proceedings of the NoDaLiDa 2017 Workshop on Processing Historical Language

edited by
Gerlof Bouma and Yvonne Adesam

22 May 2017
Gothenburg

Proceedings of the NoDaLiDa 2017 Workshop on Processing Historical Language
edited by Gerlof Bouma and Yvonne Adesam
NEALT Proceedings Series 32

Preface

The papers in this volume are presented at the Workshop on Processing Historical Language, held in conjunction with the 40-year anniversary of NoDaLiDa, 22 May 2017 in Gothenburg.

While historical texts have long attracted interest from language historians and historical linguists, we have seen an increased attention to the problems particular to processing historical data from a computational perspective in the last decade or so. 'Processing' here entails a wide range of text processing tasks, such as creating electronic transcriptions and editions of manuscripts, constructing lexica, tagging, and parsing, as well as content-oriented processing such as semantic parsing and information extraction. The aim of the workshop is to bring together researchers working on processing historical materials with a particular focus on work that investigates the combination of data-driven and knowledge-driven modelling.

We received 16 submissions, which were each reviewed (double blind) by three programme committee members. Because of the amount and quality of the submissions, the workshop, initially planned as a half-day workshop, was prolonged to accommodate 9 oral presentations.

The authors come from eight different European countries. The research presented at the workshop covers a range of topics related to historical materials, including spelling standardization, linguistic analysis, identification of text re-use, and data visualization. Featured languages are Dutch, English, Finnish, German, Icelandic, Latin, and Spanish, at varying historical stages. The programme also includes an invited talk by Stefanie Dipper, titled *Variance in historical data: how bad is it and how can we profit from it for historical linguistics?*

We are excited to have such a varied and inspiring programme and would like to thank the invited speaker, authors, and reviewers for their valuable contributions.

May 1, 2017 — Gerlof Bouma
Gothenburg — Yvonne Adesam

The workshop is organized as part of project MAÞiR – Methods for the automatic Analysis of Text in digital Historical Resources – funded by Marcus and Amalia Wallenberg Foundation, grant MAW 2012.0146.

Workshop Organization / Programme Chairs

Yvonne Adesam, University of Gothenburg
Gerlof Bouma, University of Gothenburg

Programme Committee

David Alfter, University of Gothenburg
Marcel Bollmann, Ruhr-Universität Bochum
Lars Borin, University of Gothenburg
Gosse Bouma, University of Groningen
Hanne Martine Eckhoff, University of Tromsø
Markus Forsberg, University of Gothenburg
Iris Hendrickx, Radboud University Nijmegen
Richard Johansson, University of Gothenburg
Alex Speed Kjeldsen, University of Copenhagen
Beáta Megyesi, Uppsala University
Eva Pettersson, Uppsala University
Nina Tahmasebi, University of Gothenburg
Erik Tjong Kim Sang, Meertens Institute
Marjo van Koppen, Utrecht University
Shafqat Virk, University of Gothenburg

Contents

– Invited Talk –

Variance in Historical Data: How bad is it and how can we profit from it for historical linguistics?

Stefanie Dipper
Linguistics Department
Ruhr-Universität Bochum
dipper@linguistics.rub.de

The most striking feature of historical language data is probably the amount of variance, in particular variance of spelling. For example, in a Bavarian manuscript from the 16th century, written by one author, we find eight different spellings of the word *Kreuz* 'cross':

> *creuecz, cruecz, kreevcz, kreucz, kreuecz, krevcz, krevecz, kruecz.*

If we look at the Anselm corpus 1 , which contains about 50 manuscripts and prints from different dialects of Early New High German[1] (1350–1650), there are in total 50 different spellings of that word:

> *chraewcz, chrawcz, chrawecz, chreitz, chreucz, chreuecz, chreutz, chrevcz, chrevtz, chrewcz, chrewczt, chrewecz, chrewtz, chrvtz, creucz, crecz, creuecz, creutz, cretz, crewcz, crewtz, crucz, cruecz, cruetz, cruicz, cruitz, cruiz, crutz, crtz, cruytz, crvitz, crvtz, kraitz, kreevcz, kreitz, kreucz, krecz, kreuecz, kreutz, kretz, krevcz, krevecz, krewcz, krewtcz, krewtz, krewz, krucz, kruecz, kruicz, kruitz.*

In the entire Reference Corpus of Middle High German[2] (REM, 10501350), there are 83 spelling variants of the word *Teufel* 'devil':

> *dievel, diuel, diufal, diuual, diuvil, divel, divuel, divuil, divvel, dufel, duoifel, duovel, duuel, duuil, duvel, duvil, dvofel, dvuil, dwowel, teufel, tevfel, thufel, thuuil, tiefal, tiefel, tiefil, tieuel, tieuil, tieuuel, tieuuil, tievel, tievil, tifel, tiofel, tiuel, tiufal, tiufel, tiufil, tiuil, tiuofel, tiuuel, tiuuil, tiuval, tiuvel, tiuvil, tivel, tivfel, tivil, tivuel, tivuil, tivvel, tivvil, tivwel, tiwel, tubel, tubil, tueuel, tufel, tufil, tuifel, tuofel, tuouil, tuovel, tuovil, tuuel, tuuil, tuujl, tuvel, tuvil, tvfel, tvivel, tvivil, tvouel, tvouil, tvovel, tvuel, tvuil, tvvel, tvvil, tyefel, tyeuel, tyevel, tyfel*

– minor differences, e.g., in the use of diacritics, are ignored here.

Some of the variance is due to graphemic variation (e.g., *u* vs *v* as in *crutz* vs *crvtz*). Other variants reflect phonetic differences between dialects (e.g., voiced *d* vs voiceless *t* as in *dievel* vs *tievel*).

I provide the full set of variants here to give the reader an impression of the extent and systematicity of the variance. For instance, looking at the variants of *Teufel* 'devil', we see that almost all of the individual word forms follow the general scheme:

1. They all start with a dental consonant (voiced or voiceless: *d*, *t*, *th*),
2. followed by some vowel or diphthong,
3. followed by a labiodental fricative (*u*, *v*, *w*, *f*, or combinations thereof),
4. followed by some vowel,
5. and end with *l*.

The variants of the word *Teufel* that occur in REM cover a surprisingly broad range of the forms that can be generated by the scheme above. For instance, we find *dievel* and *tievel*, but also *divel* and *tivel*, and *dvuil*, *tvuil*, and *diufal*, *tiufal*. But also *tiufal*, *tiufel*, *tiufil* and *tubel*, *tufel*, *tuuel*, *tuvel*, and so on.

In my talk, I want to present some quantitative and qualitative results of spelling variance in historical data of German, but also address variance of morphological and morpho-syntactic features to some extent.

I present two different automatic approaches of normalizing variance, by mapping it either to some artificial form or to modern German. In recent work, we have used the intermediate representations of these approaches – replacement rules and Levenshtein-based mappings – for investigating diatopic variation. First results from these investigations will be presented.

[1] `https://www.linguistics.rub.de/anselm/`
[2] `https://www.linguistics.rub.de/rem/`

Improving POS Tagging in Old Spanish Using TEITOK

Maarten Janssen
CELGA-ILTEC
maarten@iltec.pt

Josep Ausensi
Universitat Pompeu Fabra
Department of Translation and Language Sciences
josep.ausensi@upf.edu

Josep M. Fontana
Universitat Pompeu Fabra
Department of Translation and Language Sciences
josepm.fontana@upf.edu

Abstract

In this paper, we describe how the TEITOK corpus tools helped to create a diachronic corpus for Old Spanish that contains both paleographic and linguistic information, which is easy to use for non-specialists, and in which it is easy to perform manual improvements to automatically assigned POS tags and lemmas.

1 Introduction

Although the availability of computational resources for the study of language change has experienced a considerable growth in the last decade, scholars still face considerable challenges when trying to conduct research in certain areas such as syntactic change. This is true even in the case of languages for which there already exist large corpora that are freely accessible on the internet.

One of such cases is Spanish. Despite the size and quality of the textual resources available through online corpora such as CORDE[1] or the Corpus del Español[2], researchers interested in the evolution of the Spanish language cannot conduct the type of studies that have been conducted, for instance, on the evolution of the English language due to the fact that the diachronic corpora available for Spanish are scarcely annotated with the relevant linguistic information and and the range of query options is not sufficiently broad.

This presentation reports work in progress within a project that seeks to redress this situation for Spanish. Our goal is to develop resources to study the evolution of Spanish in at least the same depth as it is now possible for English. These resources have to satisfy the following requirements: (i) the texts should also contain paleographic information, (ii) they should be enriched with linguistic information (initially POS tagging and eventually also syntactic annotation), (iii) the corpus should be easy to use by non-experts in NLP, and (iv) after the initial development stage, the corpus should also be easily maintainable and improvable by non-experts in NLP. The last requirement was especially relevant in our context because the development of corpora can be a very long term process and the financial resources to hire collaborators with the necessary technical skills are not constant and are heavily dependent on grants and projects which can be difficult to obtain for corpora that have already been financed through previous grants.

Specifically, we will discuss how the TEITOK interface helped in reaching these requirements for a diachronic corpus of Spanish (OLDES). A large portion of our corpus came from the electronic texts compiled, transcribed and edited by the Hispanic Seminary of Medieval Studies (HSMS)[3]. This is a large collection of critical editions of original medieval manuscripts which comprise a wide variety of genres and extend from the 12th to the 16th centuries. The HSMS texts were turned into a linguistic corpus enriched with POS tags and lemmas in the context of the dissertation work conducted by Sánchez-Marco (Sánchez-Marco et al., 2012). The initial version of this corpus was created in a traditional verticalized set-up using the Corpus Workbench (Evert and Hardy, 2015), henceforth CWB, and was tagged using a custom built version of Freeling (Padró et al., 2010) for Old Spanish. See Sánchez et al., (2010; 2011; 2012) for a more detailed description of the corpus as well as of the problems encountered in the initial stages of development.

[1] http://corpus.rae.es/cordenet.html

[2] http://www.corpusdelespanol.org/hist-gen/

[3] See Corfis et al. (1997), Herrera and de Fauve (1997), Kasten et al. (1997), Nitti and Kasten (1997), O'Neill (1999)

2 TEITOK

The version of the corpus described here was created in the TEITOK platform (Janssen, 2015). TEITOK is an online corpus management platform in which a corpus consists of a collection of XML files in the TEI/XML format. Tokens are annotated inline, where token-based information such as POS and lemmas is modeled as attributes over those tokens. For searching purposes, an indexed version of the corpus in CWB is created automatically from the collection of XML files. With its CWB search option, TEITOK is comparable to systems like CQPWeb (Hardie, 2012), Korp (Ahlberg et al., 2013), or Bwananet (Vivaldi, 2009), with the difference that in TEITOK, the search engine additionally facilitates access to the underlying XML documents, along the lines of TXM (Heiden, 2010).

TEITOK has several attributes that make it able to respond to the four requirements mentioned in the introduction.

(i) The files of a TEITOK corpus are encoded in TEI/XML, a format that has been used extensively for encoding paleographic information. In the TEITOK interface, this information is not just present in the source code, but is graphically rendered, meaning that a TEITOK document looks like a pleasant-to-read paleographic manuscript.

(ii) TEITOK has inline nodes for tokens, as in e.g. the XML version of the BNC (BNC, 2007), which can be adorned with any type of linguistic information that is traditionally encoded in a verticalized text format, such as POS tags, lemmas, dependencies relations, etc. Furthermore, it makes a distinction between orthographic words and grammatical words, where a single orthographic word can contain multiple grammatical words (and vice-versa). This allows us to keep contractions such as *del* ('of the'), while also having the option of specifying the two grammatical words that form it: *de* ('of') and *el* ('the').

(iii) The online interface of TEITOK is designed for a broad and diverse audience, adding several features to make the corpus more easily accessible than traditional corpus interfaces: it provides an easy interface to search the corpus, in which it is possible to use the full CWB search language, but it also provides a simple form that will automatically generate a CWB search query behind the scenes. It also provides glosses for POS tags, eliminating the need to read through the tagset definitions.

(iv) Most relevantly for this paper, the same interface that is used for searching and viewing the corpus is also used to edit the corpus. This makes it easy for the administrators and authorized users to correct errors whenever they encounter them. There are also several tools available to make structural changes faster, which will be described in the next section.

Since philological information was removed in the CWB version of the corpus, we created the corpus again from the original files, this time keeping all the information provided in it. Since the two versions of the corpus were created independently, there are inevitably small differences between them: what counts as one token in one version sometimes counts as more than one in the other. This makes it close to impossible to import the tags from one version of the corpus to the other. As such, we used the Freeling parameters for Old Spanish that were developed as part of the original corpus, and applied them to the TEITOK version, resulting in a corpus that combines the linguistic and extralinguistic information in a single set of documents.

TEITOK allows for multiple orthographic realisations of the same word, which makes it possible to keep the paleographic form, and add a form in modernized orthography, making the corpus much more accessible to those not familiar with the old spelling forms. Since the lemmas provided by Freeling are in modern spelling, the modern spelling of the words was provided automatically (wherever possible), by looking up which current word corresponds to the POS tag and the modernized lemma. For instance, the word *rresçiban* was tagged as a present subjunctive (VMSP3P0) of *recibir* ('receive'). The modern Spanish lexicon for Freeling lists the form *reciban* for this, which was hence added as the modernized form.

Despite the efforts put into the initial tagging of the OLDES corpus, the level of accuracy was still not entirely satisfactory. The main objective in this stage of development was to improve the overall quality of the tagging. For this, we decided to follow the following strategy: we set apart a selection of texts summing up to 1 million tokens, and tagged it with the Freeling tagger for Old Spanish. We then used several techniques provided by TEITOK to manually correct errors in this gold standard part of the corpus. After correcting the major errors, we trained NeoTag (Janssen, 2012) on this gold standard corpus, and applied the trained tagger to the rest of the corpus.

3 Improving POS tags

Independently of how good a POS tagger is, incorrect tags will always be created. In the case of a closed corpus like the HSMS corpus, it quickly becomes more efficient to correct errors created by the tagger than to attempt to improve the quality of the tagger. Traditionally, tagging correction has been done by hand, either in a text editor or an XML editor. Tools to facilitate tag correction are relatively new, such as ANNIS (Krause and Zeldes, 2016) or eDictor (Feliciano de Faria et al., 2010). Unlike most of these tools, TEITOK allows editing directly from the XML interface.

The TEITOK version of the HSMS texts provides a comfortable and quick way to manually correct tagging errors. The base mode of editing in TEITOK involves clicking on a word in the text. This opens up an HTML form, where any of the attributes of the word can be modified. Although this is very helpful when encountering a single error while using the corpus, it is not very efficient for large corrections. Therefore, there are three main options to speed up corrections.

The first option is the closest to the traditional way of correcting tagging errors: it is possible to get a verticalized version of a text, in which multiple tokens can be corrected at once, while still seeing the surrounding tokens. In the verticalized version the editor can correct a token in all its different layers of representation, i.e. transcription, written form, editor form, expanded form, critical form and normalized form. It is possible to see the different forms for the same token, and this renders the whole manual correcting process easier since it is possible to compare the original with the more modernized form of the same token. The verticalized version also allows the editor to correct POS tags and lemmas at the same time.

A second option is to correct errors from the text in modernized orthography. Although words still have to be corrected individually in this way, it becomes much easier to spot errors: any word that is not modernized was not recognized by the tagger, and will have an incorrect lemma, and, most likely, an incorrect POS tag as well. In many cases, if a word was recognized, but incorrectly tagged, it will have an incorrect modernized form. This makes it possible to just look for incorrect words in modern Spanish, which are much easier to spot than errors in POS or lemma. For instance, if the previous example *rresçiban* had been incorrectly modernized as *recibían* by the system, it would have been easy to recognize it by simply looking the normalized version of the text. Thus, in these cases, there is no need to check the actual POS tag (something much harder to process), because the tag can be inferred by the actual modern form.

And finally, multiple tokens throughout the corpus can be corrected in batch mode using CWB queries. CWB can be used to search for very specific words that are frequently tagged incorrectly, and all words in the resulting KWIC list are clickable to correct any errors they contain. It is also possible to correct all matching results in one go, either by changing the lemma for all of them to a specific value, or by going through all the matches in a verticalized format. Thus, TEITOK can use the output of a CWB search to edit the underlying XML files. This provides a reliable and fast way to quickly correct the errors previously spotted on the verticalized view; sometimes an error spotted while correcting a text on the verticalized view is indicative of a more general problem that applies to the whole corpus. This renders the whole correction process faster since, by spotting a generalized error on the verticalized view, the editor can simply correct all the incorrectly tagged tokens of the whole corpus via the interface.

An example is given in figure 1, where a relatively simple query is used to identify all words starting with *rr-*, which is no longer used in current Spanish orthography. We then asked the system to edit the normalized form for all of those, where the normalized form was furthermore pre-treated automatically by replacing all double *rr* for a single *r*. This allows editing all such words in one go, independently of which XML file they appear in.

This general procedure can be enhanced via simple strategies to identify specific incorrectly tagged tokens. For instance, a recurrent incorrectly tagged token is the word *vienes*, as it is of-

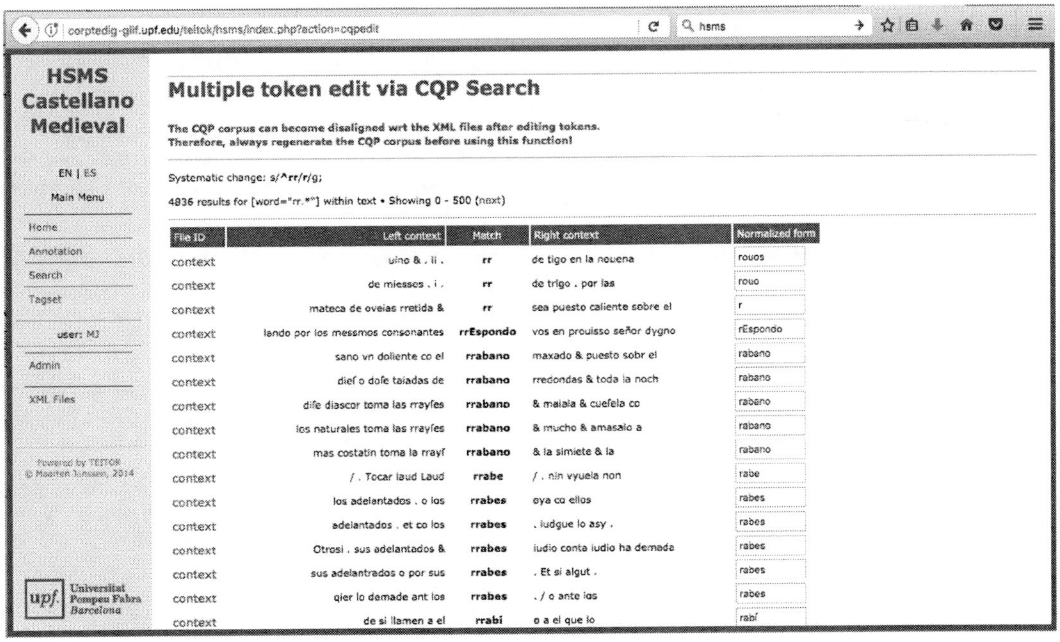

Figure 1: Multi-Editing in TEITOK

ten tagged as a verb ('you come') even though it is actually related to the modern noun spelled *bienes* ('goods'). By searching for all occurrences of the word *vienes* it is possible to correct all incorrectly marked ones in one go. It is even possible to search specifically only for occurrences of *vienes* that follow a determiner, by using a complex CQP query over multiple tokens in which the word *vienes* is marked as the target word (using the CQP operator @).

Other general problems that can be corrected automatically include examples such as the following: the form *a* is incorrectly tagged as a preposition ('to') when it relates to the modern form spelled *ha* ('he has'); the form *él* ('he') is tagged as a pronoun when it relates to the determiner *el*, or *partida* is tagged as a noun ('departure') when it relates to the participle ('departed'). All these generalized problems can be easily corrected taking advantage of the CWB interface and looking for specific combinations of the forms and specific lemmas or POS tags. For instance, searching for occurrences of *a* marked as a preposition, that are followed by a participle, gives only occurrences that should have been normalized as *ha* from the verb *haber*, hence making it possible to change all of them in batch mode. Searching for *él* followed by a noun returns instances of *él* that should have been tagged as a determiner, or searching for the lemma *ser* (i.e. be, in any form) followed by *partida* marked as a noun will return occurrences of *partida* that should have been tagged as a participle.

Since these different methods to correct errors in tags, lemmas, and normalized forms are easy to apply and do not require specific knowledge of the computational system, or imply that the corpus has to be rebuilt by a computational linguist, TEITOK allows all administrators of the corpus to correct errors over time - either by simply correcting individual errors, or by correcting multiple instances of an error throughout the corpus in batch mode as described in the previous paragraph. This means that the process of ironing out remaining errors is put back in the hands of the historical linguists, instead of requiring the technical support of external collaborators.

4 Conclusion

In this article, we hope to have shown how the TEITOK framework makes working with annotated historical corpora much easier: not only does it allow one to keep all paleographic information with the corpus, but it also makes it possible for linguists to correct annotation errors in an easy way, without the need to have detailed knowledge of the computational processes behind it. This result is a historical corpus that is useful not only for corpus linguists or syntacticians, but also, for instance, for historical linguists or philologists, and which can be improved over time, given that it is possible to correct errors whenever they are encountered. This is especially relevant in the context of historical corpora, since there are so many different sources of possible errors.

References

Malin Ahlberg, Lars Borin, Markus Forsberg, Martin Hammarstedt, Leif-Jöran Olsson, Olof Olsson, Johan Roxendal, and Jonatan Uppström. 2013. Korp and karp – a bestiary of language resources: the research infrastructure of språkbanken.

BNC. 2007. British national corpus, version 3 BNC XML edition.

Ivy A. Corfis, John O'Neill, and Jr. Theodore S. Beardsley. 1997. *Early Celestina Electronic Texts and Concordances*. Madison.

Stefan Evert and Andrew Hardy. 2015. Twenty-first century corpus workbench: Updating a query architecture for the new millennium. In *10th International Conference on Open Repositories (OR2015)*, June.

Pablo Picasso Feliciano de Faria, Fabio Natanael Kepler, and Maria Clara Paixão de Sousa. 2010. An integrated tool for annotating historical corpora. In *Proceedings of the Fourth Linguistic Annotation Workshop*, LAW IV '10, pages 217–221, Stroudsburg, PA, USA. Association for Computational Linguistics.

Andrew Hardie. 2012. Cqpweb combining power, flexibility and usability in a corpus analysis tool. *International Journal of Corpus Linguistics*, 17(3).

Serge Heiden. 2010. The TXM Platform: Building Open-Source Textual Analysis Software Compatible with the TEI Encoding Scheme. In Ryo Otoguro, Kiyoshi Ishikawa, Hiroshi Umemoto, Kei Yoshimoto, and Yasunari Harada, editors, *24th Pacific Asia Conference on Language, Information and Computation*, pages 389–398, Sendai, Japan. Institute for Digital Enhancement of Cognitive Development, Waseda University.

María Teresa Herrera and María Estela González de Fauve. 1997. *Textos y Concordancias Electrónicos del Corpus Médico Español*. Madison.

Maarten Janssen. 2012. NeoTag: a POS tagger for grammatical neologism detection. In *Proceedings of the Eighth International Conference on Language Resources and Evaluation, LREC 2012, Istanbul, Turkey, May 23-25, 2012*, pages 2118–2124.

Maarten Janssen. 2015. Multi-level manuscript transcription: TEITOK. In *Congresso de Humanidades Digitais em Portugal, Lisboa, October 8-9, 2015*.

Lloyd Kasten, John Nitti, and Wilhelmina Jonxis-Henkemans. 1997. *The Electronic Texts and Concordances of the Prose Works of Alfonso X, El Sabio*. Madison.

Thomas Krause and Amir Zeldes. 2016. Annis3: A new architecture for generic corpus query and visualization. *Digital Scholarship in the Humanities*, 31(1):118.

John Nitti and Lloyd Kasten. 1997. *The Electronic Texts and Concordances of Medieval Navarro-Aragonese Manuscripts*. Madison.

John O'Neill. 1999. *Electronic Texts and Concordances of the Madison Corpus of Early Spanish Manuscripts and Printings*. Madison.

Lluís Padró, Miquel Collado, Samuel Reese, Marina Lloberes, and Irene Castellón. 2010. Freeling 2.1: Five years of open-source language processing tools. In *Proceedings of 7th Language Resources and Evaluation Conference (LREC'10)*, La Valletta, Malta, May.

Cristina Sánchez-Marco, Gemma Boleda, and Lluís Padró. 2010. Annotation and representation of a diachronic corpus of spanish. In *Proceedings of the Language Resources and Evaluation Conference*, Malta, May. Association for Computational Linguistics.

Cristina Sánchez-Marco, Gemma Boleda, and Lluís Padró. 2011. Extending the tool, or how to annotate historical language varieties. In *Proceedings of the 5th ACL-HLT workshop on language technology for cultural heritage, social sciences, and humanities*, pages 1–9. Association for Computational Linguistics.

Cristina Sánchez-Marco, J.M. Fontana, and J. Domingo. 2012. Anotación automática de textos diacrónicos del español. In *Actas del VIII Congreso Internacional de Historia de la Lengua Española*, Universidad de Santiago de Compostela.

Jorge Vivaldi. 2009. Corpus and exploitation tool: Iulact and bwananet. In *I International Conference on Corpus Linguistics (CICL 2009), A survey on corpus-based research, Universidad de Murcia*, pages 224–239.

The Making of the Royal Society Corpus

Jörg Knappen **Stefan Fischer** **Hannah Kermes** **Elke Teich**
Sprachwissenschaft und Sprachtechnologie
Universität des Saarlandes
{j.knappen, h.kermes, e.teich}@mx.uni-saarland.de
stefan.fischer@uni-saarland.de

Peter Fankhauser
Institut für Deutsche Sprache (IDS)
fankhauser@ids-manheim.de

Abstract

The Royal Society Corpus is a corpus of Early and Late modern English built in an agile process covering publications of the Royal Society of London from 1665 to 1869 (Kermes et al., 2016) with a size of approximately 30 million words. In this paper we will provide details on two aspects of the building process namely the mining of patterns for OCR correction and the improvement and evaluation of part-of-speech tagging.

1 Introduction

The Royal Society Corpus is built in an agile process (Cockburn, 2001; Voormann and Gut, 2008) aiming for continuous improvement from the OCR'ed original texts to the annotated corpus. In this work we elaborate on some of the details of the corpus processing including our methods of OCR pattern finding and part-of-speech tagging evaluation.

2 Improving OCR Quality

The quality of OCR for historical text is a long-standing issue (Alex et al., 2012) in corpus building. We employ a pattern based approach to OCR correction, using the stream editor *sed*. In accordance with agile principles, we build the corpus repeatedly from scratch using a build script and strict versioning (a new build number is assigned to each build).

2.1 An Initial Set of Patterns

As initial set of patterns we use the list of 50,000 patterns by Underwood and Auvil (2012) encoded as an sed script. The patterns are full words and mainly geared to correct predictable substitutions like *s* to *f*, *h* to *li*, or *e* to *c*. In a next step we eliminate all patterns that are not used at all in our corpus and patterns that result in overcorrection (this includes all patterns that convert a word-final *f* into an *s*). We also change a few patterns that transform to the wrong words in the RSC (see Table 1).

pattern	original	corrected
baving	baying	having
fhe	she	the
frem	fresh	from
11th	lith	11th
liind	hind	kind

Table 1: Corrected OCR patterns.

2.2 New Patterns from Word Embeddings

In order to find additional corpus specific OCR errors we use word embeddings. The basic idea behind this approach is that misspelled words have a very similar usage context as their correctly spelled counterparts. Using the structured skip-gram approach described in Ling et al. (2015) we compute word embeddings as a 100-dimensional representation of the usage contexts. Other than the original skip-gram approach introduced in Mikolov et al. (2013), the structured skip-gram approach takes word order in the usage context into account, and thus tends to compute similar embeddings for words with similar syntactic context. Using all words with a minimum frequency of 10 we compute embeddings for 56,000 different types coming from about 190,000 tokens. The word embeddings are L2-normalized and then grouped into 2,000 clusters using k-means clustering.

In Table 2 a few selected clusters are shown.

no.	words
2	the, thle, tile, 'the, tlhe, tie, tle, thie, ofa, 'of, tihe, tthe, ttle, .the, thte, thee, .of, ithe, of-the, th-e, onl, tothe, t-he, oni, andthe, othe, fthe, thlle, onthe, atthe, to-the, *of, sthe, ttlat
16	have, been, had, has, having, already, hath, hitherto, previously, formerly, heretofore, hlave, lhave, hlad, hlas, ihave, lhad, ving, lhas, harre, hiave, 'have, 1lave, liad, 'they, bave, hlaving
24	from, fiom, firom, friom, fiomn, fiorn, 'from, fromn, firomn, ftom, srom, fiomr

Table 2: Some example clusters.

Cluster no. 24 is a pure cluster consisting entirely of the word *from* and corrupted spellings of it. We add all those spellings to the OCR correction patterns. Clusters no. 2 and 16 demonstrate that clusters do not necessarily consist of misspelled variants only, thus they cannot be used as such without manual inspection. Altogether, we derive approximately 370 corpus specific patterns from the clusters. Cluster no. 2 also gives us the confidence to interpret *tile* as a corruption of *the* and not as the genuine word *tile*.

2.3 Beyond Words: Prefixes, Suffixes, and Substrings

Sorting the patterns alphabetically reveals a lot of common prefixes in the patterns. Going from full word patterns to prefix patterns does not only lower the number of patterns but also increases their coverage of inflected and derived forms. In a similar way, there are common patterns for derivational and inflectional suffixes, specially for common endings like *-ion* or *-ing*. We show some prefix and suffix patterns in Table 3.

There are also a few patterns that are applied everywhere. Those patterns are carefully inspected such that they do not apply to otherwise correct words. We show some examples of substring patterns in Table 4.

2.4 Removing Remains of Hyphenation

We also use a special set of pattern to correct remains of hyphenation. Most of the hyphenation occurring in the original texts was already undone. Typical remains of hyphenation include hyphenation over page breaks, or cases like *trans-. parent* where a spurious full stop is added after the hyphen. We mined for the most frequent cases and created special sed patterns to repair them.

affix	patterns
circum	circllm, circnm, circtlm, circuln, circuml, circunl, circurn, circutn
experim	experilm, experiln, experilu, experiml, experinl, experinm, experirn, experitn
sub	sllb, stlb
under	ilnder, ullder, utlder
ally	allv
ing	illg, ilng, inlg, irng, itlg, itng
ion	ioil, ioll, ionn, iorn, iotn
ment	mellt, melit, mellt, merlt, metlt

Table 3: Some prefix and suffix patterns.

substring	patterns
qu	qll, qtl
spher	spllr
th	tlh, tlz, t}l, t}z
wh	vvh

Table 4: Some substring patterns.

2.5 Remaining Cases

In total, there are about 42,000 OCR corrections that are found by about 2,000 sed patterns. We show the five most frequent substitutions in Table 5.

However, not in all cases a word corrupted by OCR errors can be reconstructed reliably. We encountered cases like *llow* that can come from now or how, or *tne* that can come from me or the. In those cases we currently don't apply an automated correction. Future builds of the corpus may contain some context sensitive repair in those cases.

frequency	wrong	corrected
1346	tlle	the
1214	ofthe	of the
1140	anid	and
1093	thle	the
1032	fiom	from

Table 5: Top 5 OCR corrections.

3 Normalization

Normalization is part of the annotation step and precedes part-of-speech tagging. We chose VARD (Baron and Rayson, 2008), which detects spelling variants in historical corpora and suggests modern alternatives. It is geared towards Early Modern English an can be used semi-automatically after training. To this end, we trained it on a manually normalized subset of the corpus. In total, VARD automatically replaced 0.31% of the words by their modern spelling. The percentage of normalized words decreases strongly in later time periods (see Table 6).

time period	normalized words
1650s	1.47%
1700s	0.97%
1750s	0.25%
1800s	0.08%
1850s	0.06%

Table 6: Effect of normalization across time.

4 Part-of-Speech Tagging

We use TreeTagger (Schmid, 1994; Schmid, 1995) with the default parameter file for tokenization, lemmatization and annotation of part-of-speech (POS) information in the corpus. For the time being, we did not adapt the tagger to the historical text material by training or any other adjustment.

For evaluation we created a gold standard on a sample of 56,432 words, which were drawn from 159 texts covering all time periods. The sample was manually tagged by two annotators, who achieve an inter-annotator agreement of $\kappa = 0.94$ (Cohen's kappa). Differences (3,011 words) were reconciled after discussion and resulted in a gold standard, which we use in the evaluation.

4.1 Annotation Quality

A classic quantitative evaluation shows that compared to the gold standard TreeTagger has an accuracy of 0.94 (per token) on the sample corpus. In order to better judge the annotation quality and the reliability of the tagger, we additionally perform a detailed qualitative analysis of tagging errors. The goal is to identify typical errors of the tagger, possible regularities and error directions.

4.2 Detailed Evaluation of Tagging Results

In a first step, we calculate the F-score for each part-of-speech tag separately. This allows us to identify problematic pos-tags. In a second step, we use confusion matrices of pos-tags from the gold standard and the respective pos-tags assigned by TreeTagger. This allows us to identify regularities and error directions. As we are interested in the errors with the largest impact and for better readability we do not include all pos-tags of the Penn Treebank tagset in the second step but exclude tags with an F-score >= 0.99 as well as rarely used tags. We also collapse some of the fine-grained distinctions of the tagset.

Figure 1 shows a confusion matrix with the correct pos-tags from the gold standard on the y-axis and the pos-tag assigned by TreeTagger on the x-axis. The matrix is normalized for pos-tag frequency and allows to observe possible regularities and directions in the tagging errors.

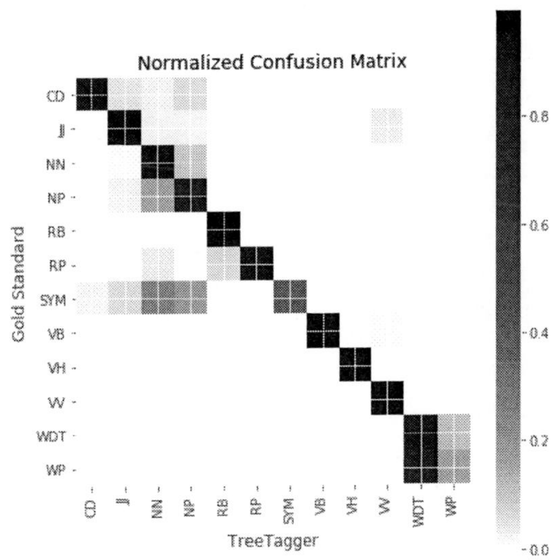

Figure 1: Normalized confusion matrix of POS annotation with the correct pos-tag on the y-axis, pos-tag assigned by TreeTagger on the x-axis.

From this we can draw the following observations. One major error source are symbols (SYM). Here we cannot really identify a direction of the errors. A closer look reveals that the pos-tag SYM is differently interpreted by the manual annotators than by TreeTagger. While the tagger assigns SYM only to single-character symbols, the annotators also tag longer words with SYM. Other error sources exhibit more obvious regularities and error directions. For example, TreeTagger often confuses common nouns (NN) with proper nouns (NP) and wh relative pronouns (WP) with wh relative determiners (WDT). In the latter case, *which*, e.g., is exclusively tagged as WDT. Although these error sources are unproblematic for a variety of linguistic annotations, they have a considerable impact on tagger performance.

The impact of the identified errors gets more obvious if we look at the confusion matrix with absolute frequencies of the pos-tags shown in Figure 2. As the figures are not normalized, only highly frequent observations are visible, and the shading is directly linked to the overall impact of the error. Thus, the error with the highest overall impact is the NN-NP error, followed by the WP-WDT and the NP-NN error. If we remove all noun related errors from the error list, tagging accuracy rises from 0.94 to 0.96.

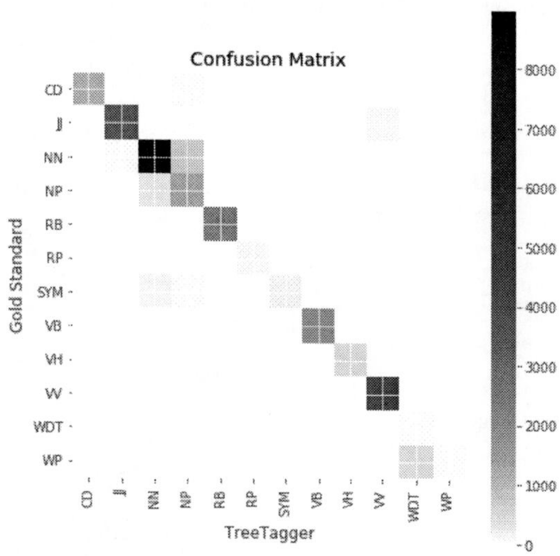

Figure 2: Confusion matrix of POS annotation with the correct pos-tag on the y-axis, pos-tag assigned by TreeTagger on the x-axis.

The NN-NP errors arise mainly from out-of-vocabulary words. While in contemporary English common nouns are always written in lower case, and capitalization indicates a proper noun, common nouns are still quite frequently capitalized in Late Modern English. Thus, a modern tagger has a strong tendency to tag capitalized words as proper nouns. We can also observe a decline of NN-NP errors over time in the RSC. Figure 3 shows the distribution of the ten most frequent tags across time. While most tags remain steady over time, the progression of NN and NP is remarkable. Their share is equal in the first two time periods (ca. 9%), then NN increases and NP decreases. Yet, the combined share of NN and NP remains the same (ca. 18%). We attribute this to the fact that in earlier time periods, capitalization of common nouns was still frequent, but decreases over time.

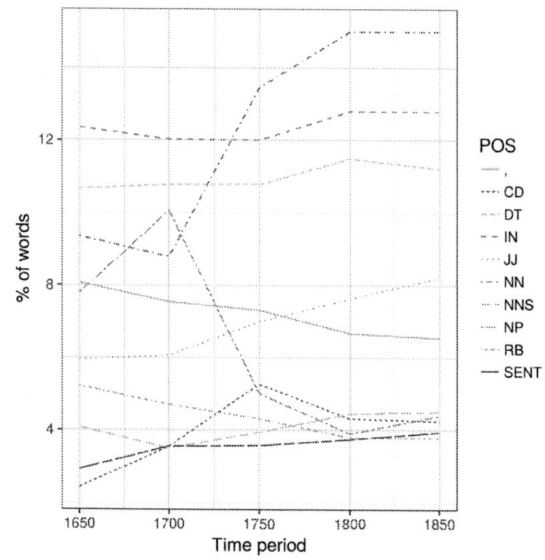

Figure 3: Most frequent POS tags across time.

4.3 Future Improvements

In order to tackle the identified typical errors, we opt for an improvement of the tagger lexicon, as we see a close relation to the major error sources. Thus, we extract all unknown words as well as all sentence internal capitalized words from the corpus. For the capitalized words, we construct lexicon entries (semi-)automatically using the tagger on the lower case version of the words. Besides, we manually construct lexical entries for frequent unknown words. Additionally, we extended the abbreviations lexicon of the tokenizer, in order to reduce segmentation errors due to unrecognized abbreviations. We extracted a list of candidate abbreviations from the corpus and checked them manually. As a result we added a list of 170 abbreviations to the tokenizer's list of abbreviations.

By the time of the workshop we will be able to present results of a new evaluation based on these improvements. Besides, we will also train the tagger on our data and compare the performance of both tagger versions.

5 Conclusion

We have presented an agile corpus building process to continuously improve the Royal Society Corpus. We have given details on our approach for OCR correction that may be helpful to other projects as well. We store all OCR corrections in a stream editor (sed) file that is applied to the corpus sources in each build with strict versioning. The agile approach extends to the stages of normalization and tagging where improvements are stored in parameter files for the tools we are using.

Both the general approach and some of the resources we created (like the patterns for OCR correction) can be applied to other corpus building projects.

The Royal Society Corpus (corpusBuild 2.0) has been made available for download and online query from the CLARIN-D centre at the Saarland University under the persistent identifier `http://hdl.handle.net/11858/00-246C-0000-0023-8D1C-0`. We also plan to release the OCR correction patterns in this context.

References

Bea Alex, Claire Grover, Ewan Klein, and Richard Tobin. 2012. Digitised historical text: Does it have to be mediOCRe? In *Proceedings of KONVENS 2012 (LThist 2012 workshop)*, pages 401–409, Vienna, Austria.

Alistair Baron and Paul Rayson. 2008. VARD 2: A tool for dealing with spelling variation in historical corpora. In *Proceedings of the Postgraduate Conference in Corpus Linguistics*, Birmingham, UK.

Alistair Cockburn. 2001. *Agile Software Development*. Addison-Wesley Professional, Boston, USA.

Hannah Kermes, Stefania Degaetano-Ortlieb, Ashraf Khamis, Jörg Knappen, and Elke Teich. 2016. The royal society corpus: From uncharted data to corpus. In *Proceedings of the LREC 2016*, Portorož, Slovenia, May 23-28.

Wang Ling, Chris Dyer, Alan Black, and Isabel Trancoso. 2015. Two/too simple adaptations of word2vec for syntax problems. In *Proceedings of NAACL*.

Tomas Mikolov, Ilya Sutskever, Kai Chen, Greg S. Corrado, and Jeff Dean. 2013. Distributed representations of words and phrases and their compositionality. In *Advances in Neural Information Processing Systems*, pages 3111–3119.

Helmut Schmid. 1994. Probabilistic part-of-speech tagging using decision trees. In *Proceedings of International Conference on New Methods in Language Processing*.

Helmut Schmid. 1995. Improvements in part-of-speech tagging with an application to german. In *Proceedings of the ACL SIGDAT-Workshop*.

Ted Underwood and Loretta Auvil. 2012. Basic OCR correction. `http://usesofscale.com/gritty-details/basic-ocr-correction/`.

Holger Voormann and Ulrike Gut. 2008. Agile corpus building. *Corpus Linguistics and Linguistic Theory*, 4(2):235–251.

Normalizing Medieval German Texts: from rules to deep learning

Natalia Korchagina
Institute of Computational Linguistics
University of Zurich
korchagina@cl.uzh.ch

Abstract

The application of NLP tools to historical texts is complicated by a high level of spelling variation. Different methods of historical text normalization have been proposed. In this comparative evaluation I test the following three approaches to text canonicalization on historical German texts from 15th–16th centuries: rule-based, statistical machine translation, and neural machine translation. Character based neural machine translation, not being previously tested for the task of normalization, showed the best results.

1 Introduction

Due to an increased interest in Digital Humanities, more and more heritage texts are becoming available in digital format. The ever growing amount of these text collections motivates researchers to use automatic methods for its processing. In many cases, automatic processing of historical corpora is complicated by a high level of spelling variation. Non-standardized orthography, resulting in inconsistent data, is a substantial obstacle to the application of the existing NLP tools. Normalization of historical texts, i.e., the mapping of historical word forms to their modern equivalents (see Figure 1), has proven to be an effective method of improving the quality of the automatic processing of historical corpora.

SOURCE: *Witter sy im nitt zu wissen .*
NORM.: Weiter sei ihm nicht zu wissen .

Figure 1: Sentence in historical German (SOURCE) and its modernised spelling (NORM.).

Various approaches to text normalization have been proposed. For instance, methods based on the Levenshtein edit distance algorithm and its variations are widely used for text canonicalization. Bollmann et al. (2011) described a technique performing automatic Levenshtein-based rule derivation from a word-aligned parallel corpus. Pettersson et al. (2013a) presented a different string similarity approach, using context-sensitive, weighted edit distance calculations combined with compound splitting. Another approach, applying character-based statistical machine translation (SMT) is documented in (Pettersson et al., 2013b; Scherrer and Erjavec, 2013; Sánchez-Martínez et al., 2013). Pettersson et al. (2014) conducted a comparative evaluation of the following three normalization approaches: filtering, Levenshtein-based and SMT-based, to show that the latter generally outperformed the former two methods. Bollmann and Søgaard (2016) reported that a deep neural network architecture improves the normalization of historical texts, compared to both baseline using conditional random fields and Norma tool (Bollmann, 2012). Deep learning methods are known to work best with large amounts of data, and yet the authors witnessed an improvement with only a few thousand tokens of training material.

Considering the above mentioned successful applications of both character-based SMT and neural networks for normalization of historical texts, I explore the suitability of character-based neural machine translation for this task. Costa-Jussà and Fonollosa (2016), and Lee et al. (2016) presented character-based neural MT systems improving machine translation. Moreover, compared to the deep learning architecture described in (Bollmann and Søgaard, 2016), a neural MT system does not require an explicit character alignment, which makes the normalization setup easier.

This paper reports the results of a comparative evaluation of normalization methods applied to Early New High German texts (1450–1550).

For this assessment I tested the following normalization methods: edit-based, statistical machine translation, and neural machine translation. The first two approaches were previously tested on German texts from the same period, but the application of neural MT to text normalization has not yet been documented. Section 2 introduces the data used for the experiments. In Section 3, I will describe the normalization methods. Section 4 will present evaluation results. Finally, in Section 5 I will summarize the outcome of the comparative evaluation and give some possible direction for future work.

2 Historical Text Corpora

This study is part of a larger project funded by the Swiss Law Sources Foundation, where I use historical legal texts[1] (i.e., decrees, regulations, court transcripts) kindly provided by the Foundation as material for my research. Therefore, I am particularly interested in finding the best performing method for normalizing these historical texts. The Collection of the Swiss Law Sources is multilingual and contains texts issued on Swiss territory from the early Middle Ages up to 1798. In my research project I work with texts written between 1450 and 1550, which corresponds to the Early New High German period. Available in digital format as critical editions of the primary sources (i.e., manuscripts), they do not contain any linguistic annotation or normalized forms. For this case study, we manually normalized a subset of the corpus, 2500 historical-modern word pairs. This dataset will be referred to as baseline in this paper.

The baseline dataset being considerably small, I also augmented it with other historical German data, to observe, if the amount of training data influences normalization results.

First, I added the data from the database of historical terms of the Swiss Law Sources Foundation. The German part of this database covers the period from 1220 to 1798. The database contains historical terms situated at the end of each printed volume of the Foundation, as well as modern keywords, corresponding to the source terms. I extracted 16,857 historical-modern pairs for normalization experiments. This corpus, due to its provenance, i.e., dictionary of terms, mostly contains nouns. In the next sections, I will refer to this dataset as LemmData.

[1] `https://www.ssrq-sds-fds.ch/online/`

Another corpus to augment the training set, is a manually annotated subset of the GerManC corpus (Scheible et al., 2011), containing 50,310 historical-modern word pairs belonging to the time period 1650–1800 (Early Modern German), and to the following eight genres: drama, newspapers, sermons, personal letters, narrative prose, scholarly, scientific and legal text.

The additional datasets, LemmData and GerManC, are quite different from the baseline. The LemmData corpus is closer to the baseline geographically, being produced on the Swiss territory, but it covers a much larger temporal span. GerManC is the largest corpus of the three, but it belongs to a much later period and was produced mainly on the German territory. Given the areal diversity of historical German, the regional provenance of GerManC contributes to its difference from the baseline. Nevertheless, by now, it is the only publicly available corpus of historical German containing manually produced normalizations. To measure the spelling variance present in the three datasets, I calculated the average string distance. For the baseline corpus, LemmData, and GerManC it corresponds to 0.91, 2.36, and 0.32, respectively. The biggest amount of spelling variation is thus present in the LemmData corpus. This can be explained by the following two facts. First, some of its lexicon belongs to the earliest period of the three texts (13th century). Furthermore, in contrast to the other two datasets consisting of regular texts, the LemmData corpus is based on a dictionary of terms. It mostly contains nouns, and does not include any punctuation marks.

The datasets' details are summarized in Table 1.

3 Normalization Methods

3.1 The Norma tool

The Norma tool[2] was developed for (semi-)automatic normalization of historical corpora. It was originally created for canonicalization of Early New High German texts, but can be trained on any data. The tool comes with three external modules, "normalizers", each implementing a normalization method. These modules can be used either separately or combined. The normalizers provide normalization candidates. Depending on how the candidate's confidence score compares to a pre-defined

[2] `https://github.com/comphist/norma`

Corpus	Period	Pairs	Region	Genres	Content	Av. LD
baseline	1463-1538	2500	CH: Bern	legal texts	text	0.91
LemmData	1220-1798	16,857	CH: all German speaking Swiss cantons	legal texts	dictionary	2.36
GerManC	1650-1800	50,310	DE: North, West Central East Central West Upper East Upper	drama newspapers sermons personal letters narratives scientific texts legal texts	text	0.32

Table 1: Corpora used in this case study.

threshold, Norma decides, whether this candidate is acceptable.

The three normalizers are: *Mapper*, *RuleBased*, and *Weighted Levenshtein Distance*. *Mapper* uses a simple wordlist mapping method. The *RuleBased* normalizer uses context-aware rules automatically derived from aligned training data, to rewrite sequences of the input characters. More details on this approach can be found in (Bollmann et al., 2011). The *Weighted Levenshtein Distance* normalizer finds a candidate with the lowest weighted Levenshtein distance score.

Since the mapping method is conceptually simple, I will not be using it in this case study. For the evaluation, I tested the remaining two normalizers separately and combined, to find out the combination where the *RuleBased* normalizer followed by *Weighted Levenshtein Distance* works best. This setup will be referred to as *Norma* in further sections.

3.2 Statistical Machine Translation

As a second method for this case study, I used character-level statistical machine translation. It differs from word-level machine translation in that it aligns characters occurring in token pairs, instead of aligning words. As a result, translation models contain phrases consisting of character sequences instead of word sentences. Language models, in their turn, are trained on character n-grams instead of word n-grams.

For the SMT experiments, I used the Moses toolkit[3] with settings as described in (Pettersson et al., 2013b).

[3] http://www.statmt.org/moses/

3.3 Neural Machine Translation

The recently proposed approach to machine translation, neural MT (Bahdanau et al., 2014; Sutskever et al., 2014; Luong et al., 2015; Cho et al., 2014) obtained state-of-the-art results for various language pairs. Neural MT systems are generally implemented as an encoder-decoder architecture. The encoder reads the source sentence and encodes it into a sequence of hidden states, whereas the decoder generates a corresponding translation based on the encoded sequence of hidden states.

I did not find any reports on the application of neural MT to the task of historical text normalization, but the comparative study by Sennrich (2016) proved that a fully character-level neural MT model outperformed a fully subword model at transliterating unknown names. This task is similar to normalization. The fully character-level neural MT approach in these experiments which I followed in mine, is described in (Lee et al., 2016).

This method maps a source character sequence to a target character sequence without explicit segmentation. Due to the fact that this model has no explicitly hard-coded knowledge of word boundaries, it is possible to use sentence-aligned data for training and testing. Nevertheless, since part of my data, i.e., LemmData is not a set of sentences, but a set of historical-modern pairs, I use tokenized, word-aligned datasets for neural MT experiments as well.

The source code implementing the models described by Lee et al. (2016) is publicly available[4].

[4] https://github.com/nyu-dl/dl4mt-c2c

4 Evaluation

Given the small size of the manually normalized baseline (2500 historical-modern word pairs), I applied 10-fold cross-validation to evaluate the performance of the three normalization methods. First, the experiments were conducted on the baseline, with 2000 pairs (2250 for Norma) of training data, 250 pairs in development set (for SMT and neural MT), and 250 pairs in the test set. Then, the training set was augmented with LemmData and GerManC data, while using both development and test sets in their initial size. Table 2 shows the evaluation results.

The neural MT system trained on the baseline combined with LemmData and GerManC (69,167 tokens) showed the best accuracy score, 0.81. It is followed by SMT results, 0.79, trained on 18,857 tokens of the baseline augmented with LemmData.

To estimate the average variability in the output between the folds of test data, I calculated the standard deviation of the accuracy for each system (SD_{acc} in Table 2). This measure demonstrates how close or far away the data is from the mean (average accuracy, ACC in Table 2). It approximates the mean distance between each fold and the arithmetic mean. The majority of the data (68.2% assuming that the distribution is normal) would be located between one standard deviation above and below the mean. For instance, given the average accuracy 0.75 of the Norma baseline system, the standard deviation 0.03 means that the accuracy scores for the majority of the folds vary from 0.72 to 0.78. The standard deviation between different systems changes slightly, from 0.02 to 0.04.

It is interesting to observe, how the systems respond to the augmentation of the training set (see Figure 2). While the performance of the rule-based system, Norma, remains rather stable, it changes by the other two systems. The SMT system first reacts positively to the increase of the training data with LemmData. This data is similar to the baseline in its regional provenance, though is very varied with respect to the covered time periods (see Table 1). When the training set was further augmented with GerManC, belonging to a later period of time, it resulted in a performance decrease. On the other hand, the performance of the neural MT system steadily increased with each addition of data. This observation corresponds to the one made in (Bollmann and Søgaard, 2016) where the normalization accuracy increased with a deep learning normalization method and remained stable or decreased with other methods, including Norma.

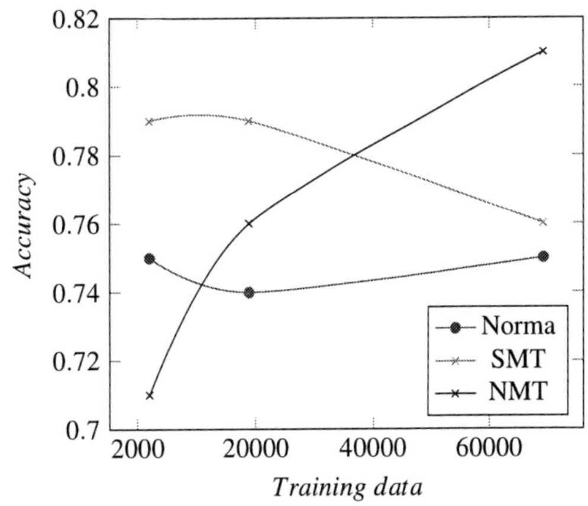

Figure 2: Word accuracy averaged over 10 folds for different sizes of the training set.

The accuracy and character error rate scores of the three normalization systems compared in the best performing configurations does not differ much: from Norma's 0.75/0.14 to neural MT's 0.81/0.08. To estimate how different the output of the systems actually is, I conducted a quantitative analysis of the output (see Table 3). First, I compared how similar is the output of the systems, i.e., how often the systems agree on a certain normalization. The lowest, 70%, is the agreement between the three systems, and the highest, 80%, between the SMT and the neural MT systems. In addition, based on the amount of the commonly incorrect cases, I calculated the percentage of the "error agreement", i.e., how often the systems produced the same erroneous normalization. The pair SMT/neural MT leads with 51% of error similarity. Thus, the output produced by SMT and neural MT systems is the most similar. It can be explained by the statistical nature of both systems, in contrast to the rule-based Norma.

Table 4 presents contrastive examples of the output, where one system produced the correct normalization, and the other two failed.

5 Conclusion

I presented a comparative evaluation of the approaches to spelling normalization in historical texts, tested on Early New High German data (1450-1550). I tested the following three meth-

Training data	Pairs	Norma			SMT			NMT		
		ACC	CER	SD_{acc}	ACC	CER	SD_{acc}	ACC	CER	SD_{acc}
baseline	2000	0.75	0.14	0.03	0.79	0.08	0.03	0.71	0.17	0.04
baseline+LemmData	18,857	0.74	0.14	0.03	0.79	0.08	0.03	0.76	0.11	0.04
baseline+LemmData+GerManC	69,167	0.75	0.13	0.02	0.76	0.10	0.04	0.81	0.08	0.03

Table 2: Averaged evaluation results, i.e., accuracy (ACC) and character error rate (CER) over 10 folds.

Systems	Agreement	Common incorrect normalizations
Norma & SMT & NMT	70%	46%
Norma & SMT	76%	44%
Norma & NMT	75%	35%
SMT & NMT	80%	51%

Table 3: Analysis of the output: total amount of cases the systems agreed upon (Agreement) and amount of cases where the systems produced the same incorrect normalization, calculated based on the number of common incorrect cases.

SOURCE	Norma	SMT	NMT	REF
meyen	maien	mein	mai	mai
ander	ander	andere	ander	andere
sturen	steuern	sturen	steueren	steuern

Table 4: Normalization examples. Correct normalizations are highlighted.

ods: rule-based, character-level statistical machine translation, and character-level neural machine translation. In this case study, neural MT outperformed the other two methods. In contrast to the rule-based method and SMT, it also benefited most from the augmentation of the training set.

Considering the success of the applied neural method, future work may consist in testing other deep learning methods. For instance, I used only one of the systems presented in (Lee et al., 2016), the fully character-based one. The other described a system performing neural machine translation with subword units.

Another direction for future work could consist in adding more training data to observe, if the performance of the neural MT system would continue to improve.

More effort could also be invested into the SMT method. The SMT system did not profit from the augmentation of the training set, due to its period and domain differences from the baseline. This is similar to the problem of the out-of-domain data in phrase-based machine translation. Out-of-domain data introduces ambiguity to the translation model, resulting in the translation choices irrelevant for the test set. Translation model domain adaptation approach was proposed by Sennrich (2012) to deal with the out-of-domain data. This method can potentially improve the results of the SMT experiments with additional training sets.

Acknowledgments

The author would like to thank Dr. Pascale Sutter and Rebekka Plüss for normalizing the source data used in the experiments as baseline. This work is supported by the Swiss Law Sources Foundation.

References

Dzmitry Bahdanau, Kyunghyun Cho, and Yoshua Bengio. 2014. Neural machine translation by jointly learning to align and translate. *CoRR*, abs/1409.0473.

Marcel Bollmann and Anders Søgaard. 2016. Improving historical spelling normalization with bi-directional LSTMs and multi-task learning. In *Proceedings of COLING 2016, the 26th International Conference on Computational Linguistics: Technical Papers*, pages 131–139, Osaka, Japan, December. The COLING 2016 Organizing Committee.

Marcel Bollmann, Florian Petran, and Stefanie Dipper. 2011. Rule-based normalization of historical texts. In *Proceedings of Language Technologies for Digital Humanities and Cultural Heritage Workshop*, pages 34–42.

Marcel Bollmann. 2012. (Semi-)automatic normalization of historical texts using distance measures and the Norma tool. In *Proceedings of the Second Workshop on Annotation of Corpora for Research in the Humanities (ACRH-2)*, Lisbon, Portugal.

Kyunghyun Cho, Bart van Merrienboer, Dzmitry Bahdanau, and Yoshua Bengio. 2014. On the properties of neural machine translation: Encoder-decoder approaches. *CoRR*, abs/1409.1259.

Marta R. Costa-Jussà and José A. R. Fonollosa. 2016. Character-based neural machine translation. *CoRR*, abs/1603.00810.

Jason Lee, Kyunghyun Cho, and Thomas Hofmann. 2016. Fully character-level neural machine translation without explicit segmentation. *CoRR*, abs/1610.03017.

Minh-Thang Luong, Hieu Pham, and Christopher D. Manning. 2015. Effective approaches to attention-based neural machine translation. *CoRR*, abs/1508.04025.

Eva Pettersson, Beáta Megyesi, and Joakim Nivre. 2013a. Normalization of historical text using context-sensitive weighted Levenshtein distance and compound splitting. In *Proceedings of the 19th Nordic Conference on Computational Linguistics*.

Eva Pettersson, Beáta Megyesi, and Jörg Tiedemann. 2013b. An SMT approach to automatic annotation of historical text. In *Proceedings of the Workshop on Computational Historical Linguistics at NODALIDA*.

Eva Pettersson, Beáta Megyesi, and Joakim Nivre. 2014. A multilingual evaluation of three spelling normalisation methods for historical text. In *Proceedings of the 8th Workshop on Language Technology for Cultural Heritage, Social Sciences, and Humanities (LaTeCH)*, pages 32–41, Gothenburg, Sweden, April. Association for Computational Linguistics.

Felipe Sánchez-Martínez, Isabel Martínez-Sempere, Xavier Ivars-Ribes, and Rafael C. Carrasco. 2013. An open diachronic corpus of historical Spanish: annotation criteria and automatic modernisation of spelling. *CoRR*, abs/1306.3692.

Silke Scheible, Richard J. Whitt, Martin Durrell, and Paul Bennett. 2011. A gold standard corpus of Early Modern German. In *Proceedings of the 5th Linguistic Annotation Workshop*, LAW V '11, pages 124–128, Stroudsburg, PA, USA. Association for Computational Linguistics.

Yves Scherrer and Tomaž Erjavec. 2013. Modernizing historical Slovene words with character-based SMT. In *BSNLP 2013 - 4th Biennial Workshop on Balto-Slavic Natural Language Processing*, Sofia, Bulgaria, August.

Rico Sennrich. 2012. Perplexity minimization for translation model domain adaptation in statistical machine translation. In *EACL 2012, 13th Conference of the European Chapter of the Association for Computational Linguistics, Avignon, France, April 23-27, 2012*, pages 539–549.

Rico Sennrich. 2016. How grammatical is character-level neural machine translation? Assessing MT quality with contrastive translation pairs. *CoRR*, abs/1612.04629.

Ilya Sutskever, Oriol Vinyals, and Quoc V. Le. 2014. Sequence to sequence learning with neural networks. In *Advances in Neural Information Processing Systems 27: Annual Conference on Neural Information Processing Systems 2014, December 8-13 2014, Montreal, Quebec, Canada*, pages 3104–3112.

Ambiguity in Semantically Related Word Substitutions: an investigation in historical Bible translations

Maria Moritz **Marco Büchler**
Institute of Computer Science
University of Goettingen
mmoritz@gcdh.de mbuechler@etrap.eu

Abstract

Text reuse is a common way to transfer historical texts. It refers to the repetition of text in a new context and ranges from near-verbatim (literal) and para-phrasal reuse to completely non-literal reuse (e.g., allusions or translations). To improve the detection of reuse in historical texts, we need to better understand its characteristics. In this work, we investigate the relationship between para-phrasal reuse and word senses. Specifically, we investigate the conjecture that words with ambiguous word senses are less prone to replacement in para-phrasal text reuse. Our corpus comprises three historical English Bibles, one of which has previously been annotated with word senses. We perform an automated word-sense disambiguation based on supervised learning. By investigating our conjecture we strive to understand whether unambiguous words are rather used for word replacements when a text reuse happens, and consequently, could serve as a discriminating feature for reuse detection.

1 Introduction

Detecting text reuse is an important means for many scholarly analyses on historical texts. Nonetheless, the detection of para-phrasal reuse in historical texts is not yet well understood. Specifically, techniques borrowed from plagiarism detection (Alzahrani et al., 2012) are quickly challenged when words are substituted.

To improve historical text-reuse detection, we need to better understand the characteristics of reuse–such as the way and the ratio of word substitutions and modifications. We also need to learn about the characteristics of words that are often substituted to identify potential features that automated

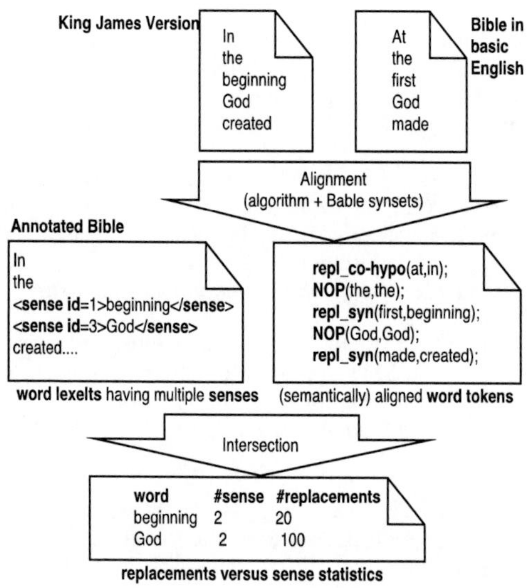

Figure 1: Methodology overview

reuse-detection techniques can take into account. In earlier work, we already investigated the ratios and modifications (morphological and semantic) in two smaller corpora of ancient text. In this paper, we investigate ambiguous words from an upfront word-sense annotated English Bible, and compare them with word substitutions that we find between the verses of this and two further English Bibles each. Since in historical text, text reuse is a way to transfer knowledge, we conjecture that words that are substituted in a para-phrasal, reused verse (of a para-phrasal, parallel corpus) are less likely ambiguous words and do not have multiple senses. We are inspired by Shannon's (1949) conditional entropy, which measures the ambiguity of a received message, i.e., the missing information of a message compared to what was actually sent (cf. Borgwaldt et al., 2005). We conjecture that ambiguous words are likely less specific (informative) and are no good candidates for a substitution (for a reused text in our case).

Fig. 1 illustrates our methodology. First, we determine the intersection of the ambiguous words from the first (word-sense-annotated) Bible and the replaced words between this Bible and the two other Bibles. Second, we disambiguate the two extra Bibles using a k-nearest neighbors classifier and a support vector machine classifier (based on the training data of the annotated Bible) and intersect the ambiguous words found that way (now knowing their numbers of senses as well) again with the replacements collected from the first step, to back-up our findings.

2 Related Work

Some works consider semantic information for detecting text smilarity. Sanchez-Perez et al. (2014) discover sentence similarity based on a tf-idf weighting during text alignment that allows them to keep stop words without increasing the rate of false positive hits in the result set. Their recursive algorithm allows to increase the alignment up to a maximal passage length. By using synset databases, Bär et al. (2012) consider semantic similarity in addition to structural features (e.g., n-grams of POS sequences) and stylistic characteristics (e.g., sentence and word length). They empirically show that taking their suggested wide variety of textual features into account works best to detect text reuse. Their method outperforms previous methods on every dataset on which their method was tested.

Fernando and Stevenson (2008) present an algorithm that identifies paraphrases by using word-similarity information derived from WordNet (Fellbaum, 1998). They experiment with several measures for determining the similarity of two words represented by their distance in the WordNet's hierarchy. Their methods turned out to work slightly better than early works did—to which their methods are compared to.

Some works also consider the influence of word ambiguity for plagiarism detection. Ceska and Fox (2011) investigate whether ambiguous words impact the accuracy of their plagiarism-detection technique. Among others, they examine the removal of stop words, lemmatization, number replacement and synonym recognition, and how they affect accuracy. They find that number replacement, synonym recognition, and word generalization can slightly improve accuracy.

We want to find out about the role of ambiguous words in a reuse scenario to define new requirements for text-reuse detection methods in historical text as a long-term goal.

3 Study Design

We now describe our study design, including our research question, datasets, and tools that we used.

3.1 Research Question

We formulate one research question:

RQ1. *Is there a correlation between words that are often replaced during text reuse and words that are unambiguous (i.e., have one sense only)?*

In other words, we ask whether unambiguous words are more frequently substituted than ambiguous words in reused text. We think that unambiguous words are more likely replacement candidates in a text that is reused, because thy probably transport clearer information. This can depend on the reuse motivation (e.g., the reason to create an edition). However, we want to learn if we can find a trend that follows our conjecture.

3.2 Datasets

We use three English Bibles. The first is the King James Version (KJV) from 1611–1769. It has been annotated with word senses. The other two Bibles are the Bible in Basic English (BBE)—1941–1949—and Robert Young's Literal Translation (YLT). YLT from 1862 very literally follows the Hebrew and Greek language. Because these Bibles follow different linguistic criteria, they offer a greater lexical diversity. We consider both Bibles as the counterpart of the text reuse (target text), and the KJV as source text.

To obtain word senses for the latter two Bibles, we use the word senses of KJV as training data for a machine-learning task, which we then apply to both BBE and YLT.

3.3 Methodology

Our methodology comprises three steps.

1) We identify word substitutions pairwise between KJV and BBE, and between KJV and YLT. Therefore, we align words of a Bible verse hierarchically by first associating identical words and words wich have the same lemma in common, and then we look for synonym, hypernym, hyperonym, and co-hyponym relations between the words of two Bible verses, which we use BabelSenses (Navigli and Ponzetto, 2012), for.

2) We then compare the annotated words (multi- and single-sense words) of the sense-annotated

Bible	tokens	types
KJV	967,606	15,700
BBE	839,249	7,238
YLT	786,241	14,806

Table 1: General lexical information on the corpus

KJV with the substituted words from the former step (cf. Fig. 1).

3) Finally, we identify word senses in both BBE and YLT using a k-nearest neighbors classifier and a support vector machine classifier trained with the KJV annotations, and do the same comparison as in step 2 to see whether our conjecture still holds or not, or only holds for the new replacement words in BBE and YLT.

Step 2 and 3 rely on annotated training data that was created for KJV by Reganato et al. (2016).[1] They used BabelNet synsets (Navigli and Ponzetto, 2012) to identify semantic concepts and disambiguate words using the word sense disambiguation (WSD) system Babelfy (Moro et al., 2014). They performed semantic indexing on their Bible corpus after disambiguation and entity-linking. To evaluate the Babelfy output, they manually annotated two chapters of their Bible. The confidence score of the annotations is between 70%–100%.

4 Ambiguity in Replaced Words

Next, we investigate if words substituted between Bibles are rather unambiguous than ambiguous.

4.1 Data Preparation and Corpus Overview

Because of the age of KJV (18th century), we use MorphAdorner (Paetzold, 2015) for its lemmatization. We use the lemma output from TreeTagger (Schmid, 1999) for both BBL and YLT. We use the lemmas to query the BabelNet API to find synonyms, hypernyms, hyponyms and cohyponyms for a given word. We query BabelNet to find synonyms, hypernyms, hyperonyms, and cohyponyms presenting potential replacements when we compare the Bible verses. For orientation, Table 1 gives an overview of the Bible vocabulary, and Table 2 shows information on the annotation data. Both tables show raw information on the given corpora.

[1] `http://homepages.inf.ed.ac.uk/s0787820/bible`

KJV annotated single-word lexelts	9,927
KJV annotated multi-word lexelts	2,794
total	12,721

Table 2: Information on annotated KJV Bible

4.2 Replacement Statistics

We first calculate the words that are substituted by another word, pairwise between each KJV and BBE, and between KJV and YLT. In Table 3 we list an overview of types and tokens of words containing relations such as synonyms, hyponyms, hypernyms, and co-hyponmys. In total, we find **4,172** lexelts (words that have one or multiple meanings) of the annotated KJV in the intersection with BBE and **3,312** lexelts in the intersection with YLT.

In the following, we show and explain diagrams of the results on these intersections. We relate the number of replacement operations of lexelts to the number of their senses. Note that the y-axis is logarithmic to compress the data points for clarity. In Fig. 2 we normalize the number of replacements between KJV and BBE by the number of senses, with the result that—judged by the box and median values—relatively above a sense number of four, the increase of the number of replacement operations stagnates a bit. This behavior is confirmed in Fig. 3, which shows the replacement operations between KJV and YLT by sense numbers of the replaced lexelts, again relative to the number of senses. Here, a strong increase is visible from four and six senses on (based on box and median).

5 Word Sense Disambiguation Task

Now, we investigate whether we obtain a similar result when we automatically disambiguate the word

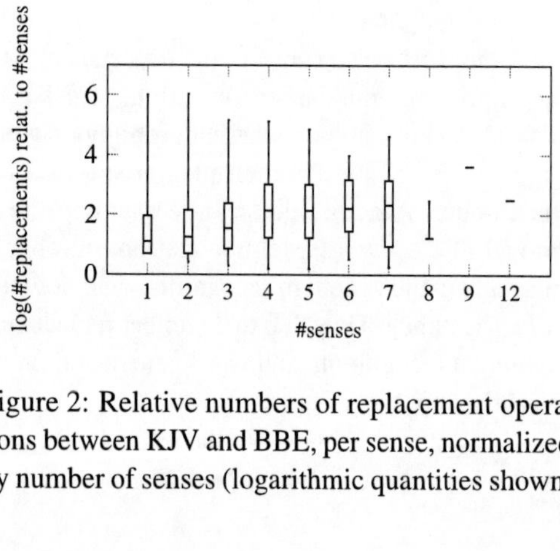

Figure 2: Relative numbers of replacement operations between KJV and BBE, per sense, normalized by number of senses (logarithmic quantities shown)

source Bible	target Bible	subst. types source B.	subst. types target B.	subst. tokens
KJV	BBE	4,947	2,048	150,938
KJV	YLT	3,915	4,094	74,851

Table 3: Substitution statistics between the Bibles

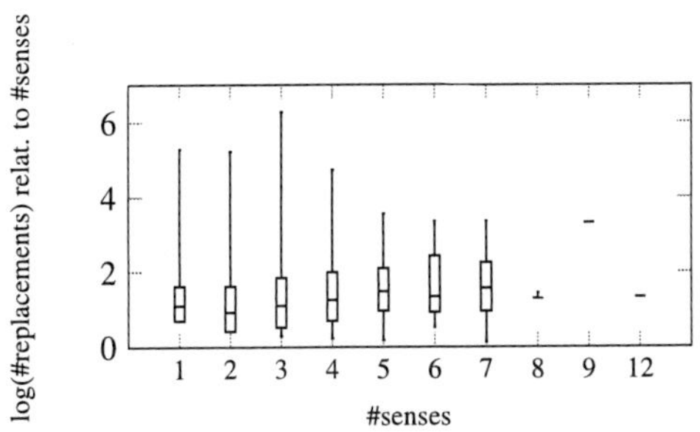

Figure 3: Relative numbers of replacement operations between KJV and YLT, per sense, normalized by the number of senses (logarithmic quantities displayed)

senses using two different machine learning classifiers.

5.1 Preparation of the Experiment

To obtain an understanding of the classifiers' accuracy, we first evaluate them using the given annotation data: we split the 66 files representing the Bible (one book per file) randomly into two thirds for training and one third for testing. We train and test two classifiers (explained shortly). We use three filter criteria for the testing data: i) all word and sense classes are only considered in the testing data if they also appear in the training data; ii) only words (lexelts) with at least two different senses are considered, and iv) only words with at least 30 instances per sense are considered. We choose 30 as the instance threshold, because we work with a 20-tokens-window feature space, thus feature matrices turn out sparse. On the other hand, we want to loose as few words as possible. Table 4 shows the baseline accuracy of this preparatory test, before we run the classifiers on our two other Bibles.

classifier	p	r	correct	attempted	total
KNN	.678	.670	8317	12266	12408
SVM	.679	.672	8334	12266	12408

Table 4: Performance—(p)recision and (r)ecall—of the KNN and SVM on the annotated test data

Classifiers Used: We use two classifiers from the sklearnpackage: the Linear Support Vector Classifier (SVM) and the KNeighbors Classifier (KNN). For the latter, we leave the number of neighbors and the weight at their default value. Table 4 shows the classifiers' ground performance on the training and testing data set from the annotated KJV Bible.
Error Rates per Sense Number: We further calculate the averaged error per sense number for both classifiers on the test data. Table 5 shows the results for the sense number 2, 3 and 4.

5.2 Substitutions in two Automatically Annotated Bibles

Now, we want to identify word senses in the two extra Bibles as well. For performing the WSD analysis on the BBE and the YLT, we use all Bible books of the annotated KJV Bible as training data (but again use only lexelts with at least 30 instances per sense to remain comparable), and the two classifiers already used before.

We find **88** lexelts contained in the intersection set. Next, we describe the results of the intersection. We intersect the words classified by SVM and KNN with the words that were replaced among BBE and KJV. Fig. 4 shows the results. The output of the classified word senses from both, KNN and SVM are intersected with the same replacement operations identified in the previous section. Fig. 4 shows the replacements for both classifiers' output. Again, the ratio of replacements seems to stagnate starting with a sense number of 5 (cf. Sec. 4.2 for information on replaced types and tokens between BBE and KJV, and YLT and KJV).

Next, we run the same procedure using substituted words between YLT and KLV. We find **138** lexelts in the intersection Fig. 5 interestingly shows

classifier	no. of senses		
	2	3	4
KNN	.47	.62	.74
SVM	.46	.60	.70

Table 5: Averaged classification error per sense number for the KNN and SVM classifier

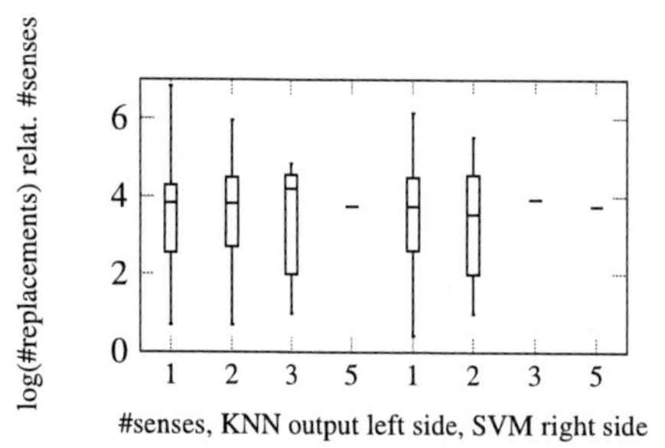

Figure 4: Relative numbers of replacement operations between BBE and KJV, per sense, normalized by number of senses (logarithmic quantities shown)

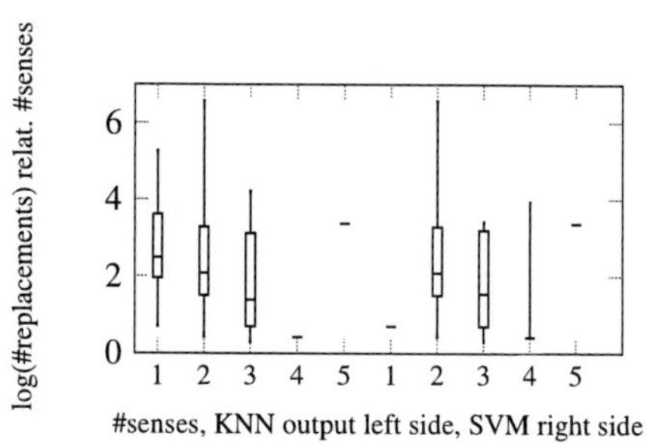

Figure 5: Relative numbers of replacement operations between YLT and KJV, per sense, normalized by number of senses (logarithmic quantities shown)

a decrease of replacements with an increase of the sense number of a word for results found using the KNN classifier. This can be explained by the closeness of YLT's language to the ancient, original text, and that its words in some contexts are less commonly used. Thus, words are substituted between YLT and KJV where none are substituted in between BBE and KJV, e.g.:

- repl_syn(sons,children) in [YLT,KJV], but NOP(children,children) in [BBE,KJV] (cf. Psalm 45:16)
- repl_syn(flames,fire) in [YLT,KJV], but NOP(fire,fire) in [BBE,KJV] (cf. Psalm 57:4)
- repl_syn(prepared,fixed) in [YLT,KJV], but NOP(fixed,fixed) in [BBE,KJV] (cf. Psalm 57:7)
- hypo(honour,glory) in [YLT,KJV], but NOP(glory,glory) in [BBE,KJV] (cf. Psalm 57:8)

Thus, they are good candidates for a replacement in a more common, even if older, translation as it is KJV. The calculated results using the SVM classifier, however, do not show statistically reliable data (too few data points for words with 1, 4 and 5 senses). Hence, we can not form an outcome based on them.

6 Threats to Validity

External Validity: A threat is that the word senses annotated in the King James Version of the Bible are generated from Babel Senses and the Word Sense Disambiguation system Bablelfy. Both use BabelNet synsets as the underlying knowledge base. Since we also use BabelNet to identify semantic relationships between two words of two Bible verses, we possibly find our conjecture influenced negatively from the beginning, because a unique word sense might never be given when its meaning is harvested by means of context vectors, which use a specific, surrounding context. This threat might be overcome in future work. A broader hand-annotated sense inventory together with a WSD classification task might be chosen instead of the given annotated Bible.

Internal Validity: A threat is that we can only find intersections with words that were successfully lemmatized upfront and for which we can find an entry in BabelNet. A lemma lookup failed in 6,210 cases for the BBE Bible and in 11,312 cases for the YLT Bible. No corresponding counterpart for a token was found 139,565 times for the intersection of KJV with BBE, and 83,285 times for YLT. Lemma lookups often failed when words contained special characters (such as "'s") due to a lemma-list cleaning we performed, or when a named entity was not used in both verses, and a lowercase version could not be found. Especially in the automated annotated data we encounter low data points. In the future we want to experiment with different thresholds to find a good setting between recall and precision.

Finally, we intentionally do not call our conjecture hypothesis, since we do not perform hypothesis testing using statistical tests, mainly since the results do not indicate that our conjecture holds. We are currently exploring other potential, discriminating features. Upon indications that they hold, we will perform statistical hypothesis testing.

7 Discussion

Our results show that—against the initial conjecture—the likeliness of a word being replaced correlates to its number of senses (shown by the fact that—even though normalized—boxes in Fig. 2 to Fig. 5 tend to raise instead of fall). There is no conspicuousness in the use of unambiguous words as potential substitution candidates in a parallel para-phrasal corpus, such as the one used in this paper. Thus, if a word is unambiguous, it is no discriminating criteria for a word to be a potential candidate for replacements in a reuse situation. As mentioned in Sec. 6, this possibly relies on the selection of the resources we use to find semantic relatives (e.g., synonyms) for the words in our parallel Bible corpus.

However, we found an interesting discrimination in the second part of our experiment. It turned out that between the YLT and the KJV indeed more unambiguous words are in the replacement set. This might be influenced by the fact that YLT contains much more types when much fewer tokes were replaced at the same time (cf. Table 3).

Moreover, we only tested the conjecture on one genre (the Bible), whereas it might be possible that other sorts of text reuse behave differently, which also might be a further aspect to investigate.

8 Conclusion

We showed whether and how (ambiguous) words—when substituted—correlate to the number of their senses. In contrast to our initial conjecture, there is no significance in the use of unambiguous words as replacements candidates. Instead, the use of a word as a substitution candidate for para-phrasal reuse increases with the number of the senses of a word. In future work, we strive to compare word substitutions to another sense annotated dataset and to define the ambiguity by a word's appearance in only one or multiple synonym sets directly. In any case, we will further investigate the characteristics of words from reused text to derive more understanding on how text is constituted when reused.

Acknowledgments

Our work is funded by the German Federal Ministry of Education and Research (grant 01UG1509).

References

Salha M. Alzahrani, Naomie Salim, and Ajith Abraham. 2012. Understanding plagiarism linguistic patterns, textual features, and detection methods. *Trans. Sys. Man Cyber Part C*, 42(2):133–149.

Daniel Baer, Torsten Zesch, and Iryna Gurevych. 2012. Text reuse detection using a composition of text similarity measures. In *Proceedings of COLING 2012*, pages 167–184, Mumbai, India. The COLING 2012 Organizing Committee.

Susanne R Borgwaldt, Frauke M Hellwig, and Annette M B De Groot. 2005. Onset entropy matters–letter-to-phoneme mappings in seven languages. *Reading and Writing*, 18(3):211–229.

Zdenek Ceska and Chris Fox. 2011. The influence of text pre-processing on plagiarism detection. Association for Computational Linguistics.

Christine Fellbaum. 1998. *WordNet An Electronic Lexical Database*. MIT Press.

Samuel Fernando and Mark Stevenson. 2008. A semantic similarity approach to paraphrase detection. *Computational Linguistics UK (CLUK 2008) 11th Annual Research Colloqium.*

Andrea Moro, Alessandro Raganato, and Roberto Navigli. 2014. Entity linking meets word sense disambiguation: A unified approach. *Transactions of the Association for Computational Linguistics*, 2:231–244.

Roberto Navigli and Simone Paolo Ponzetto. 2012. Babelnet: The automatic construction, evaluation and application of a wide-coverage multilingual semantic network. *Artif. Intell.*, 193:217–250, December.

GH Paetzold. 2015. Morph adorner toolkit: Morph adorner made simple.

Alessandro Raganato, Jose Camacho-Collados, Antonio Raganato, and Yunseo Joung. 2016. Semantic indexing of multilingual corpora and its application on the history domain. In *Proceedings of the Workshop on Language Technology Resources and Tools for Digital Humanities (LT4DH)*, pages 140–147, Osaka, Japan. The COLING 2016 Organizing Committee.

Miguel A Sanchez-Perez, Grigori Sidorov, and Alexander F Gelbukh. 2014. A winning approach to text alignment for text reuse detection at pan 2014. In *CLEF (Working Notes)*, pages 1004–1011.

Helmut Schmid. 1999. Improvements in part-of-speech tagging with an application to german. In *Natural language processing using very large corpora*, pages 13–25. Springer.

Claude E Shannon. 1949. Communication theory of secrecy systems. *Bell Labs Technical Journal*, 28(4):656–715.

The Lemlat 3.0 Package for Morphological Analysis of Latin

Marco Passarotti
CIRCSE Research Centre
Università Cattolica del Sacro Cuore
marco.passarotti@unicatt.it

Marco Budassi
Università degli Studi di Pavia
marcobudassi@hotmail.it

Eleonora Litta
CIRCSE Research Centre
Università Cattolica del Sacro Cuore
eleonoramaria.litta@unicatt.it

Paolo Ruffolo
CIRCSE Research Centre
Università Cattolica del Sacro Cuore
paolo.ruffolo@posteo.net

Abstract

This paper introduces the main components of the downloadable package of the 3.0 version of the morphological analyser for Latin Lemlat. The processes of word form analysis and treatment of spelling variation performed by the tool are detailed, as well as the different output formats and the connection of the results with a recently built resource for derivational morphology of Latin. A light evaluation of the tool's lexical coverage against a diachronic vocabulary of the entire Latin world is also provided.

1 Introduction

A sector of the research area dealing with linguistic resources and Natural Language Processing (NLP) tools that has seen a large growth across the last decade is the one dedicated to building, sharing and exploiting linguistic resources and NLP tools for ancient languages. This has particularly concerned Latin and Ancient Greek as essential means for accessing and understanding the so-called Classical tradition.

Although Latin was among the first languages to be automatically processed with computers (thanks to the pioneering work done by the Italian Jesuit Roberto Busa since the late '40s), throughout history, computational linguistics has mainly focused on living languages. However, the start, in 2006, of the first two syntactically annotated corpora (*treebanks*) for Latin[1] gave rise to a kind of renaissance for linguistic resources and NLP tools for ancient languages.

Several textual and lexical resources, as well as NLP tools, are currently available for Latin. Given that out-of-context lemmatisation and morphological analysis of word forms are generally considered basic layers of linguistic analysis - in some way, feeding the subsequent ones - different morphological analysers were developed for Latin across the years. These are: *Words* (`http://archives.nd.edu/words.html`), Lemlat (`www.lemlat3.eu`), *Morpheus* (`https://github.com/tmallon/morpheus`), reimplemented in 2013 as *Parsley* (`https://github.com/goldibex/parsley-core`), the PROIEL Latin morphology system (`https://github.com/mlj/proiel-webapp/tree/master/lib/morphology`) and *LatMor* (`http://cistern.cis.lmu.de`). *Morpheus*, *Parsley* and *LatMor* are all capable of analysing word forms into their morphological representations including vowel quantity.

Although Lemlat has proved to be the best performing morphological analyser for Latin together with LatMor[2] and the one provided with the largest lexical basis (in terms of both selection of the lexicographic sources and processing of attested graphical variants), its impact on the research community has been narrowed for years by its limited accessibility. Only recently, the tool was made freely available, in its 3.0 version,

[1] These were the *Index Thomisticus* Treebank, based on texts of Thomas Aquinas (IT-TB; Passarotti, 2009) and the Latin Dependency Treebank (LDT; Bamman and Crane, 2006), on texts of the Classical era. Later on, a third Latin treebank was made available in the PROIEL corpus (Haug and Jøndal, 2008), which includes the oldest extant versions of the New Testament in Indo-European languages and Latin texts from both the Classical and Late eras. All the three Latin treebanks are dependency-based.

[2] For the results of a comparison between the morphological analysers for Latin see Springmann et al. (2016, p. 389).

thanks to the collaboration between the CIRCSE Research Centre in Milan and the Istituto di Linguistica Computazionale of CNR in Pisa (ILC-CNR). This paper introduces the main components of the downloadable package of Lemlat 3.0.

2 Lemlat

First released as a morphological lemmatiser at the end of the 1980s at ILC-CNR (v 1.0; Bozzi and Cappelli, 1990; Marinone, 1990) and there enhanced with morphological features between 2002 and 2005 (v 2.0; Passarotti, 2004), Lemlat relies on a lexical basis resulting from the collation of three Latin dictionaries (GGG: Georges and Georges, 1913-1918; Glare, 1982; Gradenwitz, 1904) for a total of 40,014 lexical entries and 43,432 lemmas, as more than one lemma can be included in one lexical entry.

Lemlat was originally built for performing the automatic lemmatisation of the texts in the collection of Latin grammarians by Heinrich Keil (1855-1880). Since the first version of Lemlat, one desideratum was pursuing a philological approach to lexical data, which was addressed by connecting the lexical basis of the tool with widely recognised reference dictionaries for Latin, whose contents where collated and recorded carefully. In the light of such an approach, Georges and Georges (1913-1918) was chosen instead of Forcellini's *Lexicon Totius Latinitatis* (1940). Indeed, although Forcellini is the Latin dictionary that comprises the highest number of lemmas, Lomanto (1980) demonstrates that Georges and Georges shows both a higher lexical richness and a better quality of the entries.

Given that Forcellini is the Latin dictionary providing the largest Onomasticon, in the context of the development of the 3.0 version of Lemlat, its lexical basis was further enlarged by adding semi-automatically most of the Onomasticon (26,415 lemmas out of 28,178) provided by the 5th edition of Forcellini (Budassi and Passarotti, 2016).[3]

2.1 Word Form Analysis

Given an input word form that is recognised by Lemlat, the tool produces in output the corresponding lemma(s) and a number of tags conveying (a) the inflectional paradigm of the lemma(s) (e.g. first declension noun) and (b) the morphological features of the input word form (e.g. singular nominative), as well as the identification number (N_ID) of the lemma(s) in the lexical basis of Lemlat.[4] No contextual disambiguation is performed.

For instance, receiving in input the word form *acrimoniae* 'pungency', Lemlat outputs the corresponding lemma (*acrimonia*, N_ID: a0417), the tags for its inflectional paradigm (N1: first declension noun) and those for the morphological features (feminine singular genitive and dative; feminine plural nominative and vocative).

Lemlat is based on a database that includes several tables recording the different formative elements (segments) of word forms. The most important table is the "lexical look-up table", whose basic component is the so-called LES ("LExical Segment"). The LES is defined as the invariable part of the inflected form (e.g. *acrimoni* for *acrimoni-ae*). In other words, the LES is the sequence (or one of the sequences) of characters that remains the same in the inflectional paradigm of a lemma (hence, the LES does not necessarily correspond either to the word stem or to the root).

Lemlat includes a LES archive, in which LES are assigned an N_ID and a number of inflectional features among which are a tag for the gender of the lemma (for nouns only) and a code (called CODLES) for its inflectional category. According to the CODLES, the LES is compatible with the endings (called SF, "Final Segment") of its inflectional paradigm, which are collected in a separate table in the database of Lemlat. For example, the CODLES for the LES *acrimoni* is N1 (first declension nouns) and its gender is F (feminine). The word form *acrimoniae* is thus analysed as belonging to the LES *acrimoni* because the segment *–ae* is recognised as an ending compatible with a LES with CODLES N1.

Segmenting a word form into the structure LES + SF (*acrimoni-ae*) is just one of the possible options provided by Lemlat. Indeed, on one side, word forms can be analysed without any segmentation like in the case of uninflected words (e.g. *semper* 'always'). On the other side, more complex segmentation structures can be at work, including several different segments. This is the case, for instance, of the word form *castigatissimusque* 'and the most punished' (literal translation), which is segmented by Lemlat into *castig-at-issim-us-que*, where *castig* is a LES (for the

[3] For details about credits of the different versions of Lemlat see http://www.lemlat3.eu/about/credits/.

[4] The tagset of Lemlat is compliant with EAGLES (http://www.ilc.cnr.it/EAGLES/browse.html).

verb *castigo*, 'to punish'), *at* and *issim* are two SM ("Middle Segments") representing the infix respectively for perfect participle (*–at–*) and superlative degree (*–issim–*), *us* is a SF (singular masculine nominative) and the enclitics *que* is a SPF ("Post Final Segment"). Overall, the segmentation of *castigatissimusque* has the structure LES+SM+SM+SF+SPF. Each kind of segment is stored in a specific table in the database of Lemlat.

Finally, if the analysed word is morphologically derived or if it is the basis of one or more morphologically derived word(s), its derivation cluster is provided (see Section 3). For instance, the input word form *amabilem* is analysed by Lemlat as singular masculine/feminine accusative of the adjective *amabilis* 'lovable'. This lemma is part of a derivation cluster: *amabilis* is derived from the verb *amo* 'to love' and it is the basis for two derived words, namely the noun *amabilitas* 'loveliness' and the adjective *inamabilis* 'unlovely'. Relations are connected with the specific word formation rule they instantiate. For instance, *amabilis* is stored as a second class deverbal adjective with suffix *-a-bil-is*.

2.2 Spelling Variation

Textual material written in Latin is spread across a diachronic span wider than two millennia. Furthermore, Latin texts are distributed all over Europe and cover various kinds of genres.

Such a situation makes Latin a language featuring a large amount of spelling variations, due to several reasons, among which are the influence of local dialects, the writing conventions (which are subject to changes across time and place), as well as the style and the level of education of the authors.

Since its first version, Lemlat was designed to address the question of spelling variation. As mentioned above, one distinctive feature of Lemlat is its strict connection with the reference lexicographic sources. Such a connection motivates also the treatment of graphical variants in Lemlat. Indeed, the lexical look-up table featuring the list of LES includes also those that are used by the tool for processing spelling variations.

In the lexical look-up table, each lexical entry in dictionaries corresponds to as many lines as are the different LES required by Lemlat to process its full inflectional paradigm, spelling variations included. All lines belonging to the same lexical entry are assigned the same N_ID.

For instance, Glare (1982) records the Faliscan spelling variation *haba* for the first declension noun *faba* 'horse-bean'. In the lexical look-up table of Lemlat, this results into two separate lines with the same N_ID. One line reports the LES *fab* (for *faba*). The other has the LES *hab* (for *haba*). Both the LES are assigned a code for gender (feminine) and the same CODLES (N1). A specific field in the table is reserved for selecting the LES to use for building the lemma in the case of lexical entries featuring more than one LES. For *faba*, the LES *fab* is the one used, as the lemma in Glare (1982) is *faba* (and not *haba*).

Along with recording different LES for the same lexical entry, there is also another strategy used by Lemlat to process spelling variations. In the case of variations that apply to sets of words sharing some graphical properties, a field in the look-up table records a code that permits to alter the LES while processing the data. For instance, a large number of words including the prefix *trans–* have forms featuring graphical variations of *trans–*, namely *tra–* and *tras–* (*trans–* is the citation form of the prefix reported by Glare, 1982). In Lemlat, there are 35 lexical entries showing this spelling variation. All their LES are assigned a specific code (`t02`) in the lexical look-up table, which permits the alternation between the graphical forms of *trans–*. An example is the lemma *transfero* 'to transport'. Although its LES is *transfer*, the presence of `t02` makes Lemlat able to process also the graphical variants *trafero* and *trasfero*.

Such an approach to spelling variation is at the same time a pro and a con. On one side, it makes Lemlat lexicologically motivated, as only those variations that are recorded in the reference dictionaries are processed by the tool. On the other, it makes Lemlat rigid, as it allows to process only those graphical variants that are explicitly recorded in the lexical look-up table.

3 Derivational Morphology

The analysis of inflectional morphology provided by Lemlat has been recently enhanced with information on derivational morphology. Built within the context of an ongoing project funded by the EU Horizon 2020 Research and Innovation Programme (under the Marie Skłodowska-Curie Individual Fellowship), *Word Formation Latin* (WFL) is a derivational morphology resource for Latin that can also work as an NLP tool, thanks to its strict relation with Lemlat (Litta et al., 2016).

In WFL the lemmas of Lemlat are connected by Word Formation Rules (WFRs). In WFL, there are two main types of WFRs: (a) derivation and (b) compounding. Derivation rules are further organised into two subcategories: (a) affixal, in its turn split into prefixal and suffixal, and (b) conversion, a derivation process that changes the Part of Speech (PoS) of the input word without affixation.

WFL is built in two steps. First, WFRs are detected. Then, they are applied to lexical data. Affixal WFRs are found both according to previous literature on Latin derivational morphology (e.g. Fruyt, 2011; Jenks, 1911) and in a semi-automatic manner. The latter is performed by extracting from the list of lemmas of Lemlat the most frequent sequences of characters occurring on the left (prefixes) and on the right (suffixes) sides of lemmas. The PoS for WFRs input and output lemmas as well as their inflectional category are manually assigned. Further affixal WFRs are found by comparison with data. So far, 244 affixal WFRs have been detected: 94 prefixal and 150 suffixal.

Compounding and conversion WFRs are manually listed by considering all the possible combinations of main PoS (verbs, nouns, adjectives), regardless of their actual instantiations in the lexical basis. For instance, there are four possible types of conversion WFRs involving verbs: V-To-N (*claudo* → *clausa*; 'to close' → 'cell'), V-To-A (*eligo* → *elegans*; 'to pick out' → 'accustomed to select, tasteful'), N-To-V (*magister* → *magistro*; 'master' → 'to rule'), A-To-V (*celer* → *celero*; 'quick' → 'to quicken'). Each compounding and conversion WFR type is further filtered by the inflectional category of both input and output. For instance, A1-To-V1 is the conversion WFR that derives first conjugation verbs (V1) from first class adjectives (A1).

Applying WFRs to lexical data requires that each morphologically derived lemma is assigned a WFR and is paired with its base lemma. All those lemmas that share a common (not derived) ancestor belong to the same "morphological family". For instance, nouns *amator* 'lover' and *amor* 'love', and adjective *amabilis* all belong to the morphological family whose ancestor is the verb *amo*.

WFRs are modelled as one-to-may relations between lemmas. These relations are implemented by a table in the database where they are enhanced with their attributes (type, category, affix). So far, 299 WFRs have been applied, which build 5,348 morphological families and 23,340 input-output relations.

The contents of WFL can be accessed via a web application (available at `http://wfl.marginalia.it`; Culy et al., forthcoming), which features a positive balance between potential of data extraction and simplicity, dynamism and interactivity.

The web application represents the information stored in the tables of the database as a graph. In this graph, a node is a lemma, and an edge is the WFR used to derive the output lemma from the input one (or two, in the case of compounds), along with any affix used. The graph is represented as a collection of nodes and edges, and the set of morphological families is simply the set of connected subgraphs.

Four distinct perspectives to query WFL are available from the web application:

- by WFR – the primary interest is the WFR itself. This view enables research questions on the behaviour of a specific WFR. For example, it is possible to view and download the list of all verbs derived from a noun through a conversive derivation process (e.g. *radix* 'root' → *radicor* 'to grow roots');
- by affix – it acts similarly as above, but works more specifically on affixal behaviour. For example, this perspective enables to retrieve all masculine nouns featuring the suffix *–tor* and to verify how many of them correspond to a female equivalent ending in *–trix*;
- by PoS – the primary interest is in the PoS of input and output lemmas. This view is useful for studies on macro-categories of morphological transformation, like nominalisation and verbalisation;
- by lemma – it focuses on both derived and non-derived lemmas. It supports studies on the productivity of one specific morphological family or a set of morphological families.

The results of these browsing options are of three types:

- lists of lemmas matching a query;
- derivational clusters. This type of graph represents the derivational chain for a specific lemma, which includes all the lemmas derived from the lemma selected, as well as all those the lemma is derived from;
- summaries of the application of given WFRs to different PoS and the resulting lemmas.

4 Data Processing

The database of Lemlat 3.0 is available at `https://github.com/CIRCSE/LEMLAT3`, where also a Command Line Interface (CLI) implementation of the tool for Linux, OSX and Windows can be downloaded.

In particular, two versions are made available: (a) a client version, which requires a working MySQL server (`www.mysql.com`) containing the provided database and (b) a stand-alone version, which uses an embedded version of the database. Both the client and the stand-alone versions use the same CLI interface and can be run either in interactive or in batch mode. The interactive mode provides the user with the possibility of running Lemlat on one input word form at a time, selecting the lexical basis to use for analysis (GGG only; Onomasticon only; GGG + Onomasticon). The batch mode enables to process a bunch of word forms by entering either a file featuring the list of word forms to analyse or a full text. Three different formats are available for the output: plain text, XML and Comma-Separated Values file (CSV).

The output in the form of a plain text file reports exactly the same information displayed in the interactive mode. For each analysis of a processed word form, it provides (a) the segmentation of the word form into its formative elements, (b) its morphological features and (c) its lemma(s) with the corresponding PoS.

The XML output includes the complete analysis for each processed word form organised into explicitly named elements and attributes, and can be validated against the provided DTD.

The CSV file provides just basic lemmatisation, without morphological features. Each analysed word form is assigned its lemma and PoS (with gender for nouns). If a word form is assigned more than one lemma, these are provided on separate lines.

The list of the not analysed word forms is provided in a separate plain text file with the same name of the input file and the extension ".unk".

Both in the plain text and in the XML output files, each lemma is assigned a feature coming from WFL that informs if it is morphologically simple, i.e. not derived, or complex, i.e. resulting from the application of a WFR. Each morphologically complex lemma is matched with (a) the lemma which it derives from (two lemmas, in case of compounding), (b) the type of WFR involved, (c) the input and output PoS of the WFR and (d) the affix (prefix or suffix) if present in the derivation.

5 Evaluation

In order to evaluate the lexical coverage of Lemlat 3.0 on real texts, the full list of word forms extracted from *Thesaurus Formarum Totius Latinatis* have been lemmatised (TFTL; Tombeur, 1998). Widely recognised as the reference tool *par excellence* with regard to studies of Latin lexicon, TFTL is a large diachronic database collecting the vocabulary of the entire Latin world ranging from the ancient Latin literature to Neo-Latin works. Word forms are assigned their number of occurrences in the texts of the different eras.

400,886 out of the total 554,826 different forms of TFTL were analysed by Lemlat, for a total of 489,441 analyses, returning a coverage percentage of 72.254%.[5]

However, among the 153,447 forms not analysed by Lemlat, there are prominently sequences of letters (e.g. *aaa*), numbers (e.g. *CCC*), and extremely rare word forms (e.g. *aaliza*, 1 occurrence in TFTL). Results are more reliably evaluated by looking at the number of textual occurrences of the words analysed by Lemlat, compared to the total number of occurrences in TFTL. The sum of absolute frequencies of all word forms in TFTL is 62,922,781. The sum of absolute frequencies of those analysed by Lemlat is 61,881,702. Thus, Lemlat can analyse 98.345% of the occurrences in the TFTL texts.

6 Discussion and Future Work

Lemlat processes word forms by segmentation, finding compatible connections of formative elements, which are recorded in the tables of a database. Such rigid approach to morphological processing looks quite out-of-date if compared with the most widespread techniques currently used to perform automatic morphological analysis. In particular, several finite-state packages are today available[6], which feature both large lexical coverage and high flexibility, especially when they are connected to data driven techniques for

[5] The number of analyses is higher than the number of analysed forms, because a single word form can be assigned more than one lemma.

[6] See, for instance, the Helsinki Finite-State Transducer (Lindén et al. 2009), the Stuttgart Finite-State Transducer Tools (Schmid, 2005), the OpenFST library for weighted finite-state transducers (Allauzen et al., 2007) and the Foma finite-state library (Hulden, 2009).

statistical processing with weighted transducers (Pirinen, 2015) and for inflectional class inference (Dreyer et al. 2008). Moreover, the finite-state approach makes it possible to use the same code to handle both analysis and generation.

The segmentation-based approach pursued by Lemlat is due to two main reasons.

First, despite its recent availability, Lemlat is an old tool, being conceived in the early 1980s (Marinone, 1983), a time when the finite-state turn in computational morphology was still in its infancy.[7] Actually, the process of word form analysis performed by Lemlat is quite similar to that of finite-state morphology, as they share the basic assumption that natural language words are formed of concatenated "pieces" which are compatible to each other. The formative elements recognised by Lemlat in word forms can be seen as states and their relations as directed arcs controlled by rules. Basically, Lemlat formalises the lexicon as a finite-state transducer and analyses words as sequences of compatible segments. However, two (important) differences remain: (a) Lemlat is not meant to generate morphologically well-formed words; (b) Lemlat does not include rules for constraining lexical/surface correspondences, as it treats phonological alternations just like regular sequences of explicitly recorded segments.

Second, Lemlat was primarily built to address the needs of philologists, who are more interested in processing data according to reference lexicographic sources than in having a flexible and computationally efficient tool able to perform (also) lexical generation. Indeed, one distinctive feature of Lemlat is the quality of its lexical basis, which enables the tool to process all the graphical inflectional variants attested for the lexical entries in the reference dictionaries. Although such lexical basis allows for quite a broad textual coverage (see Section 5), several lemmas belonging to different phases of Medieval Latin are still missing. For this reason and to keep supporting Lemlat with quality lexicographic sources, we plan to expand its lexical basis with all the entries of Du Cange's (1883-1887) *Glossarium Mediae et Infimae Latinitatis*.

Furthermore, while still keeping the original philological approach Lemlat is built upon, in the near future we plan to enhance it with a statistical guesser, which might process those word forms that are not recognised by Lemlat.

As mentioned, Lemlat is an out-of-context morphological analyser. The structure of the running text is lost and no contextual disambiguation of multiple analyses is performed. The current availability of annotated corpora for Latin, like the three dependency treebanks (see Section 1), made it possible to train a number of probabilistic PoS taggers and lemmatisers. For instance, two parameter files for Latin are available for TreeTagger (Schmid, 1999). One file is based on the IT-TB, while the other is built upon data joint from the three Latin treebanks. Recently, pre-trained tagging models for Latin (based on the versions of the three Latin treebanks available in Universal Dependencies 1.3; `http://universaldependencies.org/`) were provided by RDRPOSTagger version 1.2.2 (Nguyen et al., 2014) with those for other 40 languages. Tagging accuracy ranges from 90.39 for the LDT to 98.24 for the IT-TB, PROIEL standing somewhere in the middle (95.78).[8]

The large lexical coverage and the high quality of analysis provided by Lemlat can be helpful for improving the performances of PoS taggers, by enhancing the tools with a morphological lexicon that provides all the possible pairs of lemma and morphological features for each word form. For instance, such a lexicon is used in popular PoS taggers like TreeTagger and MorphoDiTa (Straková et al. 2014). Although Lemlat was conceived to analyse input words and not to generate morphologically well-formed words, the result of the analysis performed on TFTL (see Section 5) is just a morphological lexicon for Latin providing large coverage of attested word forms.

Finally, a web application of Lemlat will be made available at `www.lemlat3.eu`, enabling users to process either single words or short texts. The web application of Lemlat will be linked and merged with that of WFL, thus providing one common environment for the online processing and visualisation of both inflectional and derivational morphology of Latin.

Acknowledgements

We thank three anonymous reviewers for their valuable comments and suggestions, which helped to improve the quality of the paper.

[7] The publication that mostly contributed to start such a turn is the 1983 dissertation by Kimmo Koskenniemi on a formalism to describe phonological alternations in finite-state terms, which he called "Two-Level Morphology" (Koskenniemi, 1983). An historical overview on finite-state morphology is given by Karttunen and Beesley (2005).

[8] A survey of the accuracy of several taggers based on a corpus of Medieval Church Latin is provided by Eger et al. (2015).

References

Cyril Allauzen, Michael Riley, Johan Schalkwyk, Wojciech Skut, and Mehryar Mohri. 2007. OpenFst: A General and Efficient Weighted Finite-State Transducer Library. In *Proceedings of the Twelfth International Conference on Implementation and Application of Automata, (CIAA 2007)*, volume 4783 of *Lecture Notes in Computer Science*, pages 11–23, Springer, Prague, Czech Republic.

David Bamman and Gregory Crane. 2006. The Design and Use of a Latin Dependency Treebank. In *TLT 2006: Proceedings of the Fifth International Treebanks and Linguistic Theories Conference*, pages 67–78.

Andrea Bozzi and Giuseppe Cappelli. 1990. A Project for Latin Lexicography: 2. A Latin Morphological Analyser. *Computer and the Humanities*, 24:421–426.

Marco Budassi and Marco Passarotti. 2016. Nomen Omen. Enhancing the Latin Morphological Analyser Lemlat with an Onomasticon. In *Proceedings of the 10th SIGHUM Workshop on Language Technology for Cultural Heritage, Social Sciences, and Humanities (LaTeCH 2016)*, pages 90–94, The Association for Computational Linguistics, Berlin.

Chris Culy, Eleonora Litta, and Marco Passarotti. Forthcoming. Visual Exploration of Latin Derivational Morphology. In *Proceedings of the 30th International Conference of the Florida Artificial Intelligence Research Society (FLAIRS-30).*

Markus Dreyer, Jason R. Smith, and Jason Eisner. 2008. Latent-variable modeling of string transductions with finite-state methods. In *Proceedings of the conference on empirical methods in natural language processing*, pages 1080–1089, Association for Computational Linguistics.

Charles du Fresne Du Cange et al. 1883-1887. *Glossarium Mediae et Infimae Latinitatis*. L. Favre, Niort.

Steffen Eger, Tim vor der Brück, and Alexander Mehler. 2015. Lexicon-assisted tagging and lemmatization in Latin: A comparison of six taggers and two lemmatization methods. In *Proceedings of the 9th SIGHUM Workshop on Language Technology for Cultural Heritage, Social Sciences, and Humanities (LaTeCH 2015)*, pages 105–113.

Egidio Forcellini. 1940. *Lexicon Totius Latinitatis / ad Aeg. Forcellini lucubratum, dein a Jos. Furlanetto emendatum et auctum; nunc demum Fr. Corradini et Jos. Perin curantibus emendatius et auctius meloremque in formam redactum adjecto altera quasi parte Onomastico totius latinitatis opera et studio ejusdem Jos. Perin.* Typis Seminarii, Padova.

Michèle Fruyt. 2011. Word Formation in Classical Latin. In James Clackson (ed.), *A companion to the Latin language*. Vol. 132, pages 157–175, John Wiley & Sons, Chichester.

Karl E. Georges and Heinrich Georges. 1913-1918. *Ausführliches Lateinisch-Deutsches Handwörterbuch*. Hahn, Hannover.

Peter G.W. Glare. 1982. *Oxford Latin Dictionary*. Oxford University Press, Oxford.

Otto Gradenwitz. 1904. *Laterculi Vocum Latinarum*. Hirzel, Leipzig.

Dag T.T. Haug and Marius L. Jøhndal. 2008. Creating a Parallel Treebank of the Old Indo-European Bible Translations. In *Proceedings of the Second Workshop on Language Technology for Cultural Heritage Data (LaTeCH 2008)*, pages 27–34.

Mans Hulden. 2009. Foma: a finite-state compiler and library. In *Proceedings of the 12th Conference of the European Chapter of the Association for Computational Linguistics*, pages 29–32.

Paul Jenks. 1911. *A Manual of Latin Word Formation for Secondary Schools*. DC Heath & Company, Boston, New York etc.

Lauri Karttunen and Kenneth R. Beesley. 2005. Twenty-five years of finite-state morphology. In *Inquiries Into Words, a Festschrift for Kimmo Koskenniemi on his 60th Birthday*, pages 71–83.

Heinrich Keil. 1855-1880. *Grammatici Latini*. Teubner, Leipzig.

Kimmo Koskenniemi. 1983. *Two-level morphology: A general computational model for word-form recognition and production*. Publication 11, University of Helsinki, Department of General Linguistics, Helsinki.

Kristen Lindén, Miikka Silfverberg, and Tommi Pirinen. 2009. HFST Tools for Morphology - An Efficient Open-Source Package for Construction of Morphological Analyzers. In Cerstin Mahlow and Michael Piotrowski (eds.), *Proceedings of the Workshop on Systems and Frameworks for Computational Morphology*, volume 41 of *Lecture Notes in Computer Science*, pages 28–47, Springer, Zurich, Switzerland.

Eleonora Litta, Marco Passarotti, and Chris Culy. 2016. Formatio formosa est. Building a Word Formation Lexicon for Latin. In Anna Corazza, Simonetta Montemagni, and Giovanni Semeraro (eds.), *Proceedings of the Third Italian Conference on Computational Linguistics (CLiC–it 2016). 5-6 December 2016, Napoli, Italy*, pages 185–189, aAccademia university press, Collana dell'Associazione Italiana di Linguistica Computazionale, vol. 2.

Valeria Lomanto. 1980. Lessici latini e lessicografia automatica. *Memorie dell'Accademia delle Scienze di Torino*, 5.4.2:111–269.

Nino Marinone. 1983. A project for a Latin lexical data base. *Linguistica Computazionale*, 3:175–187.

Nino Marinone. 1990. A Project for Latin Lexicography: 1. Automatic Lemmatization and Word-List. *Computer and the Humanities*, 24:417–420.

Dat Quoc Nguyen, Dai Quoc Nguyen, Dang Duc Pham, and Son Bao Pham. 2014. RDRPOSTagger: A Ripple Down Rules-based Part-Of-Speech Tagger. In *Proceedings of the Demonstrations at the 14th Conference of the European Chapter of the Association for Computational Linguistics (EACL)*, pages 17–20.

Marco Passarotti. 2004. Development and perspectives of the Latin morphological analyser LEMLAT. *Linguistica Computazionale*, XX-XXI: 397–414.

Marco Passarotti. 2009. Theory and Practice of Corpus Annotation in the *Index Thomisticus* Treebank. *Lexis*, 27:5–23.

Tommi A. Pirinen. 2015. Using weighted finite state morphology with VISL CG-3 – Some experiments with free open source Finnish resources. In *Proceedings of the Workshop on "Constraint Grammar-methods, tools and applications" at NODALIDA 2015, May 11-13, 2015*, pages 29–33, Institute of the Lithuanian Language, Vilnius, Lithuania. No. 113. Linköping University Electronic Press.

Helmut Schmid. 1999. Improvements in part-of-speech tagging with an application to German. *Natural language processing using very large corpora*. pages 13–25, Springer.

Helmut Schmid. 2005. A Programming Language for Finite State Transducers. In *Proceedings of the 5th International Workshop on Finite State Methods in Natural Language Processing (FSMNLP 2005)*, Helsinki, Finland.

Uwe Springmann, Helmut Schmid, and Dietmar Najock. 2016. LatMor: A Latin Finite-State Morphology Encoding Vowel Quantity. In Giuseppe Celano and Gregory Crane (eds.), *Treebanking and Ancient Languages: Current and Prospective Research* (Topical Issue), *Open Linguistics* vol. 2, pages 386–392.

Jana Straková, Milan Straka, and Jan Hajič. 2014. Open-Source Tools for Morphology, Lemmatization, POS Tagging and Named Entity Recognition. In *Proceedings of 52nd Annual Meeting of the Association for Computational Linguistics: System Demonstrations*, pages 13–18.

Paul Tombeur (ed.). 1998. *Thesaurus formarum totius latinitatis a Plauto usque ad saeculum XXum*. Brepols, Turnhout.

HistoBankVis: Detecting Language Change via Data Visualization

Christin Schätzle
Department of Linguistics
University of Konstanz
christin.schaetzle@uni-konstanz.de

Michael Hund **Frederik L. Dennig**
Department of Computer Science
University of Konstanz
{michael.hund, frederik.dennig}
@uni-konstanz.de

Miriam Butt
Department of Linguistics
University of Konstanz
miriam.butt@uni-konstanz.de

Daniel A. Keim
Department of Computer Science
University of Konstanz
daniel.keim@uni-konstanz.de

Abstract

We present HistoBankVis, a novel visualization system designed for the interactive analysis of complex, multidimensional data to facilitate historical linguistic work. In this paper, we illustrate the visualization's efficacy and power by means of a concrete case study investigating the diachronic interaction of word order and subject case in Icelandic.

1 Introduction

The increasing availability of digitized data for historical linguistic research has led to an increased use of quantitative methods, with an employment of increasingly sophisticated statistical methods (Manning and Schütze, 2003; Baayen, 2008; Hilpert and Gries, 2016). However, diachronic investigations involve understanding highly complex interactions between various linguistic and extra-linguistic features and structures. Due to the complexity of this multidimensional data, significant patterns may not be uncovered or understood.

We therefore designed *HistoBankVis*, a novel visualization system which facilitates the investigation of historical change by integrating methods coming from the field of Visual Analytics (Keim et al., 2008). HistoBankVis allows a researcher to interact with the data directly and efficiently while exploring correlations between linguistic features and structures. Our system in effect consigns to history the painstaking work of finding patterns across various different tables of features, numbers and statistical significances. Rather, in our system, the researcher can first identify certain features to be investigated and within minutes can obtain an at-a-glance overview that provides information about whether interesting patterns can indeed be identified across features over time. Relevant patterns can then be further analyzed by drilling down to individual data points and new hypotheses can be generated. These hypotheses may then be tested anew with respect to a fresh look at the data. Given that historical data typically present a data sparsity problem, we also provide multiple different ways of calculating or estimating statistical significance, e.g. Euclidean distance, to deal with the small number of data points.

The efficacy of HistoBankVis is exemplified via a concrete test case, namely a syntactic investigation of the Icelandic Parsed Historical Corpus (IcePaHC, Wallenberg et al., 2011). The IcePaHC is annotated in the Penn TreeBank style (Marcus et al., 1993) and consists of 61 texts with around one million words covering all attested stages of Icelandic.

The visualization not only identifies changing syntactic features in IcePaHC ad-hoc by means of a well-structured statistical analysis process, but also supports the researcher in the generation and validation of hypotheses. Moreover, the visualization bridges the gap between annotated values, statistical analyses and the actual underlying data by providing access to the original sentences from IcePaHC during a data filter and selection process.

2 Related Work

Visualizations tailored to the analysis of historical linguistic data range from work on modal verbs within historical academic discourse (Lyding et al., 2012) to the cross-linguistic spread of new suffixes throughout mass media (Rohrdantz et al., 2012; Rohrdantz, 2014), the semantic change of word meanings (Rohrdantz et al., 2011) and the

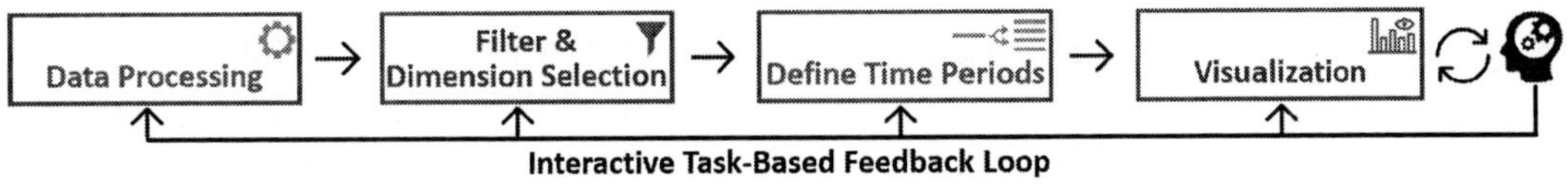

Figure 1: The workflow of our novel visualization system: based on the analysis task, the user splits documents into sentences, extracts and filters for relevant linguistic factors (=dimensions) as well as customized or pre-defined time periods. The visualization provides different levels of detail that the user can switch back and forth between. The system crucially allows for a feed-back loop by which the user can iterate back to refilter or modify the underlying data.

evolution of meanings as represented in dictionaries (Theron and Fontanillo, 2015). With respect to Icelandic and IcePaHC, Butt et al. (2014) and Schätzle and Sacha (2016) designed a glyph visualization for the analysis of individual factors leading to syntactic change. HistoBankVis builds on the experiences gathered while working on the glyph visualization. In particular, the glyph visualization was not able to deal elegantly with the potentially large amounts of interacting data dimensions that are of interest for any kind of historical linguistic research question. The system also relied on specific assumptions about the nature of the data and the research questions to be pursued.

The goal of HistoBankVis thus is to provide both a more generically applicable system for historical linguistic research and a more flexible investigation of data dimensions, allowing for exploratory access to a potentially high number of factors. The system also either provides for the possibility of analyzing each factor at a time or to look at interactions of interrelated factors on demand.

3 The HistoBankVis System

3.1 Iterative Analysis Workflow

The idea behind HistoBankVis is an iterative workflow, displayed in Figure 1. The text data are processed by extracting linguistic factors which have been identified by the researcher as relevant for the task at hand. This is typically done by a previous careful consultation of the relevant theoretical literature. In what follows, we call these linguistic factors *dimensions* and their possible values *features*. For example, the linguistic factor *voice* is a data dimension containing the features *active, passive* and *middle*. Based on the analysis task, the user can filter for a subset of the data (e.g., only certain dimensions/features or only sentences from a specific set of genres or time periods). To visualize the historical developments of dimensions over time, the researcher needs to define time periods for the comparison. The visualization then allows the researcher to interactively compare the distribution of all selected features and dimensions of the filtered sentences across the different time periods. The visualization moreover provides details-on-demand on all views via mouse interaction techniques. Finally, the user can react to the insights collected from the visualization and test new hypotheses by interacting directly with the system. Interactions could involve changes in the data processing, adapting the filters or modifying the time periods.

3.2 Data Processing

As part of a concrete case study, we are currently working with HistoBankVis to investigate the interaction between subject case and word order. Although Icelandic is generally taken to have changed only little with respect to syntax and morphology (Thráinsson, 1996; Rögnvaldsson et al., 2011), several changes with respect to word order have been documented (e.g., Kiparsky (1996), Rögnvaldsson (1996) and Hróarsdóttir (2000) on the change from OV to VO and Franco (2008) and Sigurðsson (1990) on the decrease of V1). Some questions regarding Icelandic on the basis of the existing literature are: Which strategies are used to mark grammatical relations? Do these strategies change in the history of Icelandic?

In order to investigate these questions, we identified relevant linguistic dimensions based on information contained in the theoretical literature and automatically extracted these dimensions via Perl scripts from the annotation of IcePaHC. We included information about the type of verb, voice, word order, case and valency. These dimensions were furthermore mapped onto the sentence IDs contained in IcePaHC. These sentence IDs pro-

Figure 2: The filter module: The researcher can filter for data from specific years containing only specific data features before generating a data set with previously selected dimensions.

vide information about the year date, the name and the genre of the text in which the sentence occurs. As part of our preprocessing, we used this information to generate a well-structured database that HistoBankVis can operate on.

3.3 Task-based Filtering

Once the data has been processed, the researcher has the option of filtering for sentences with relevant properties. Besides filtering for data within a specific time frame, the researcher can visually construct SQL-like filters for features in the database. Based on the analysis task, the dimensions and features can be combined with logical AND- or OR-functions. For example in Figure 2, we filtered for sentences which contain the word order OVS, i.e., (direct) object, verb, subject, within texts from 1750 to 1900 CE. The researcher then further selects the dimensions for analysis, e.g., subject case, voice, word order and the verbs involved. Each sentence matching the configured filter can be analyzed by displaying it and its Penn Treebank annotation in conjunction with all available extracted features on demand. Thus, the filtering component of HistoBankVis serves as a preprocessing system on its own, providing the researcher with a more fine-grained view on the data by only selecting a certain number of dimensions and/or a subset of sentences. This not only allows the researcher to become familiar with and explore the data set at hand, but also furthers the understanding of the data quality by granting access to detailed information about each data point. Additionally, the filtered data set can be downloaded as a CSV-file to be processed in a different tool of choice.

3.4 Analyzing Change over Time

To analyze and visualize the selected dimensions over time, the researcher has to first specify relevant time periods. For Icelandic, our system automatically supports two common divisions into time periods: (1) Old and Modern Icelandic, i.e., 1150–1550 and 1550–2008 CE (e.g., see Thráinsson (1996); referred to as *Range A* in the following); (2) more fine-grained periods as defined per Haugen (1984), i.e., 1150–1350, 1350–1550, 1550–1750, 1750-1900, and 1900–2008 CE (referred to as *Range B* in what follows). The system also allows the user to enter fully customized periods.

Compact Matrix Visualization We provide a *compact matrix* representing an understanding about differences between the selected dimensions across time periods. Each row and column of the matrix corresponds to one period.

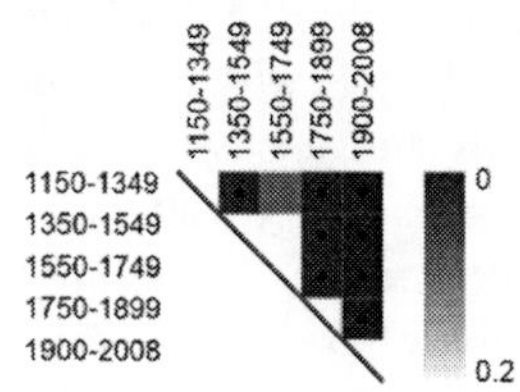

This especially facilitates the comparison of the first period to all others and every period with its predecessor (entries along the diagonal of the matrix). HistoBankVis provides two comparison modes: statistical significance and distance based. In both modes the difference between two periods is mapped onto a colormap (red depicts a high and white a low significance/distance). To measure the statistical significance, HistoBankVis supports a χ^2-test. Here the p-value is mapped to the colormap: red corresponds to $p = 0$ and white to $p \geq 0.2$. ● indicates that the difference is statistically significant (with $\alpha = 0.05$) and × signals the absence of necessary preconditions. Alternatively, the Euclidean distance can be used when the necessary preconditions for the χ^2-test are not met, e.g., in order to deal with problems of data sparsity. A high Euclidean distance reflects a large difference in the compared distributions and indicates high significance. The visual patterns in the matrix view serve as a measure of quality and "interestingness" as one can quickly spot combinations of periods which differ significantly and should be investigated further.

Difference Histograms Visualization While the overview matrix is a useful means to quickly gain insights, *difference histograms* provide a view

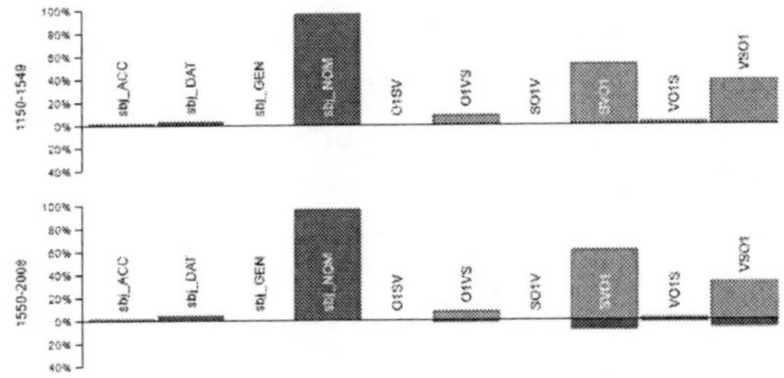

Figure 3: Difference histograms for the distribution of subject case and word order in transitive sentences in Old versus Modern Icelandic.

with more details on the diachrony of individual features. Each time period is visualized as one bar chart, see Figure 3 for Range A. Each dimension is encoded via a different color, e.g., blue for subject case and orange for word order. The height of one bar corresponds to the percentage of sentences containing the respective features. Additional information, such as the underlying sentences, the exact percentages and the relative size of the feature occurrence compared to the overall text size can be accessed via several interaction techniques.

The comparison of bar heights along different periods provides insights on which dimensions and/or combinations of features change over time. We furthermore computed the difference between two neighboring periods and visualized this as a separate bar chart below the percentages of features in the histograms. The color green indicates that a feature increased compared to the previous period and red indicates that the feature decreased, e.g., SVO increases in Figure 3, while VSO decreases. The system also allows for other comparison modes such as the option of comparing each time period with the first or last period, with the average of all periods, or with the average of all periods before the current one in order to make deviating features stand out and to observe trends.

3.5 Hypothesis Generation and Feedback ↻

Once the patterns in the data have been explored, hypotheses tested and perhaps new ones formed, the researcher can feed the knowledge gained back into each of the individual parts of the system by changing the filters, trying out different time periods or by going back to the data processing step and including different or more features. This creates an iterative analysis process in which knowledge-based and data-driven modeling are combined.

3.6 Access and Usability

HistoBankVis is implemented as an on-line browser-app and is freely available via our website.[1] The website includes a demo video which guides the user through the different analysis steps. Each analysis step performed by the user (e.g., applied filters or selected dimensions) and the current views (e.g., difference histograms) are encoded by uniquely identified URLs. The URL scheme allows a researcher to easily store and retrieve visualizations with different properties. It also allows for knowledge and data exchange between researchers supporting collaborative research projects since URLs representing a certain view on the data can be shared with other researchers locally or non-locally.

Besides the IcePaHC dataset, which HistoBankVis uses as its default data set, the system makes provision for researchers who would like to load their own data into HistoBankVis. The specifications for the new data sets are also provided. The data needs to be in a tab-separated format in which each line starts with a unique ID followed by the year date corresponding to the entry and an arbitrary number of data dimensions. Additionally, a file with meta information about the source texts (e.g., the text itself and/or the syntactically parsed sentence structure) can be uploaded as well. The mapping between the data dimensions and meta information is done via the unique ID. Further instructions and an example data set with abstract dimensions and values are available on our website, providing the user with more information on how to prepare and structure the data set.

4 Case Study

The visualizations above were obtained as part of an on-going investigation into correlations between word order and dative subjects. First, we investigated the word order distribution across all subjects in Old and Modern Icelandic by filtering for sentences containing a subject (S), a verb (V) and a direct object (O/O1). We subsequently visualized the dimensions subject case and word order. The difference histograms not only show that SVO is the dominant order for both time periods, but also that SVO is slightly increasing over time, accompanied by a concomitant decrease of VSO,

[1] `http://histobankvis.dbvis.de`

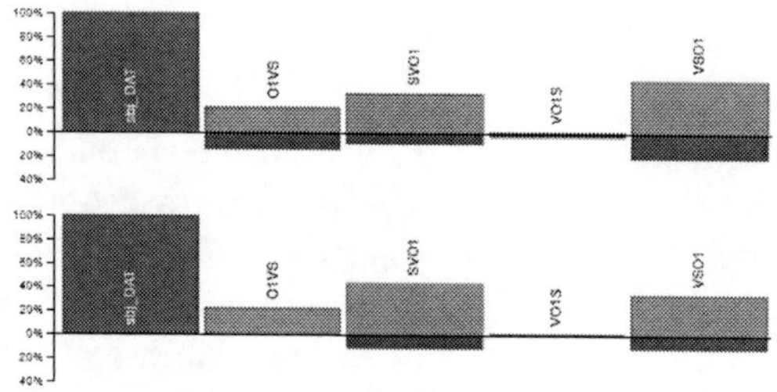

Figure 4: Word order within the past two time periods from Range B for dative subjects. See Figure 7 in the Appendix for all periods.

see Figure 3. Moreover, the subjects involved are mainly nominative and more rarely dative.

Following this initial broad look at the data, we took a more nuanced look and visualized the data with respect to Range B. Here, the distance matrix (see Section 3.4) revealed at-a-glance that there is a significant change in the last two time periods. By comparing each range with the previous one, a fairly large increase of SVO becomes visible in the last time stage (cf. the green bar under SVO1 in Figure 4), while VSO is further decreasing, as shown by the red bar underneath VSO1. Dative subjects also increase slightly in the last range (see Figure 5 in the Appendix).

Given these findings, a separate analysis of word order in dative and nominative subjects was in order. This could easily be done by configuring the filter settings to only include either dative or nominative subjects. While the word order histograms for nominative subjects (see Figure 6 in the Appendix) conform to the overall developments of word order for all subjects, dative subjects pattern differently. The difference histograms in Figure 4 show that VSO is the dominant word order for dative subject sentences until around 1900, which is when SVO surpasses VSO as dominant order following a continuous increase.

Strikingly, we found the OVS order to be standing out in the second to last time stage by deviating strongly from the average appearance in the other stages. We thus filtered the data once more for only OVS and noted that the verbs found in the relevant time period are mainly experiencer predicates, such as *líka* 'like, please', see Figure 2. We postulate that these experiencer verbs are subject to lexicalization over time and are changing from a structure in which the experiencer/goal is realized as a structural object to a structure whose sentient experiencer/goal participant is instead realized as a structural subject. I.e., something like *This pleases me*, in which the experiencer is an object is instead realized as *I like this*, where the experiencer is a subject. The general ability of experiencer/goal arguments to be realized in principle as either an experiencer subject or an undergoer/goal object has been well documented across languages (cf. Grimshaw, 1990), as have general linguistic principles by which sentient/animate participants are preferentially realized as subjects (e.g., Dowty, 1991). We postulate that the Icelandic pattern is an instance of a historical change by which experiencer participants are increasingly realized as dative subjects. Our findings are also in line with recent research on the interaction between middle morphology and dative subjects by Schätzle et al. (2015).

Recall that we also found an overall change towards SVO word order. We postulate that this points towards the development of a fixed preverbal subject position in the history of Icelandic with the 19th century as a major key turning point. Dative subjects show a slower tendency to follow this development. We explain this slower tendency by the fact that experiencer/goal arguments were not canonical subjects and that many of them underwent reanalysis from object to subject first.

Other changes with respect to Icelandic word order have been reported to happen around the same time, e.g. the decrease of V1 (Sigurðsson, 1990; Butt et al., 2014) and the loss of OV (Hróarsdóttir, 2000). These and other findings are the subject of on-going work, also with the aid of HistoBankVis. We hope to have been able to demonstrate the efficacy of HistoBankVis with this snap shot of our on-going historical work.

5 Conclusion

In conclusion, we present a powerful new visualization tool, HistoBankVis, which facilitates the detection and analysis of language change with respect to an annotated corpus. By means of just a few clicks, we were able to investigate changes in word order in interaction with subject case.

Our method combines knowledge-based and data-driven modeling. The system was developed on the IcePaHC, but has been set up in a generalized manner so that it can be applied to any Penn Treebank-style annotated corpus or indeed any annotated corpus as the visualization builds on a database designed to process any kind of well-structured data set.

HistoBankVis can also be used as a preprocessing and filtering tool without the visualization module as it allows for the export of filtered data sets. That is, the user can simply choose to filter the data set according to some features and dimensions that they specify. The user does not need to proceed on to a visualization of the selected dimensions, but can choose to export just those filtered records. If the user does choose to proceed to the visualization, the fact that the visualization is implemented as a browser-app means that each analysis step remains accessible via a single identification URL. This not only facilitates a collaborative research structure by allowing researchers to share their analyses and perspectives on the data across machines, it also facilitates the analysis process since individual perspectives on the data can be stored and individual analyses can be (re)retrieved at any time.

Finally, we hope to have demonstrated that HistoBankVis represents a novel and effective visualization system which immensely facilitates the investigation of historical language change.

Acknowledgments

We thank the German Research Foundation (DFG) for financial support within the projects A03 and D02 of the SFB/Transregio 161.

References

R. Harald Baayen. 2008. *Analyzing Linguistic Data. A Practical Introduction to Statistics Using R.* Cambridge University Press, Cambridge.

Miriam Butt, Tina Bögel, Kristina Kotcheva, Christin Schätzle, Christian Rohrdantz, Dominik Sacha, Nicole Dehe, and Daniel Keim. 2014. V1 in Icelandic: A multifactorical visualization of historical data. In *Proceedings of the LREC 2014 Workshop "VisLR: Visualization as added value in the development, use and evaluation of Language Resources"*, Reykjavik, Iceland.

David Dowty. 1991. Thematic proto-roles and argument selection. *Language*, 67(3):547–619.

Irene Franco. 2008. V1, V2 and criterial movement in Icelandic. *Studies in Linguistics*, 2:141 – 164.

Jane Grimshaw. 1990. *Argument Structure*. The MIT Press, Cambridge.

Einar Haugen. 1984. *Die skandinavischen Sprachen: Eine Einführung in ihre Geschichte.* Hamburg: Buske.

Martin Hilpert and Stefan Th. Gries. 2016. Quantitative approaches to diachronic corpus linguistics. In Merja Kytö and Päivi Pahta, editors, *The Cambridge Handbook of English Historical Linguistics*, pages 36–53. Cambridge University Press, Cambridge.

Thorbjörg Hróarsdóttir. 2000. *Word Order Change in Icelandic. From OV to VO.* John Benjamins, Amsterdam.

Daniel Keim, Gennady Andrienko, Jean-Daniel Fekete, Carsten Görg, Jörn Kohlhammer, and Guy Melançon. 2008. Visual analytics: Definition, process, and challenges. In *Information visualization*, pages 154–175. Springer.

Paul Kiparsky. 1996. The shift to head-initial VP in Germanic. In H. Thráinsson, J. Peter, and S. Epstein, editors, *Comparative Germanic Syntax*. Kluwer.

Verena Lyding, Stefania Degaetano-Ortlieb, Ekaterina Lapshinova-Koltunski, Henrik Dittmann, and Christopher Culy. 2012. Visualising linguistic evolution in academic discourse. In *Proceedings of the EACL 2012 Joint Workshop of LINGVIS & UNCLH*, pages 44–48. Association for Computational Linguistics.

Christopher D. Manning and Hinrich Schütze. 2003. *Foundations of Statistical Natural Language Processing*. The MIT Press, Cambridge, 6 edition.

Mitchell P. Marcus, Mary Ann Marcinkiewicz, and Beatrice Santorini. 1993. Building a large annotated corpus of English: the Penn Treebank. *Computational Linguistics*, 19(2):313–330.

Eiríkur Rögnvaldsson, Anton Karl Ingason, and Einar Freyr Sigurðsson. 2011. Coping with variation in the Icelandic Parsed Historical Corpus (IcePaHC). In J.B. Johannessen, editor, *Language Variation Infrastructure*, volume 3 of *Oslo Studies in Language*, pages 97–112.

Eiríkur Rögnvaldsson. 1996. Word order variation in the VP in Old Icelandic. *Working Papers in Scandinavian Syntax*, 58:55–86.

Christian Rohrdantz, Annette Hautli, Thomas Mayer, Miriam Butt, Frans Plank, and Daniel A. Keim. 2011. Towards Tracking Semantic Change by Visual Analytics. In *Proceedings of ACL 2011 (Short Papers)*, pages 305–310.

Christian Rohrdantz, Andreas Niekler, Annette Hautli, Miriam Butt, and Daniel A. Keim. 2012. Lexical Semantics and Distribution of Suffixes - A Visual Analysis. *Proceedings of the EACL 2012 Joint Workshop of LINGVIS & UNCLH*, pages 7–15, April.

Christian Rohrdantz. 2014. *Visual Analytics of Change in Natural Language*. Ph.D. thesis, University of Konstanz.

Christin Schätzle and Dominik Sacha. 2016. Visualizing language change: Dative subjects in Icelandic. In Annette Hautli-Janisz and Verena Lyding, editors, *Proceedings of the LREC 2016 Workshop "VisLR II: Visualization as Added Value in the Development, Use and Evaluation of Language Resources"*, pages 8–15.

Christin Schätzle, Miriam Butt, and Kristina Kotcheva. 2015. The diachrony of dative subjects and the middle in Icelandic: A corpus study. In M. Butt and T. H. King, editors, *Proceedings of the LFG15 Conference*. CSLI Publications.

Halldór Ármann Sigurðsson. 1990. V1 declaratives and verb raising in icelandic. In Joan Maling and Annie Zaenen, editors, *Modern Icelandic Syntax (Syntax and Semantics 24)*, pages 41–69. Academic Press, San Diego.

Roberto Theron and Laura Fontanillo. 2015. Diachronic-information visualization in historical dictionaries. *Information Visualization*, 14(2):111–136.

Höskuldur Thráinsson. 1996. Icelandic. In Ekkehard König and Johan van der Auwera, editors, *The Germanic Languages*, pages 142–189. Routledge, London.

Joel C. Wallenberg, Anton Karl Ingason, Einar Freyr Sigurðsson, and Eiríkur Rögnvaldsson. 2011. Icelandic Parced Historical Corpus (IcePaHC). Version 0.9.

Appendix

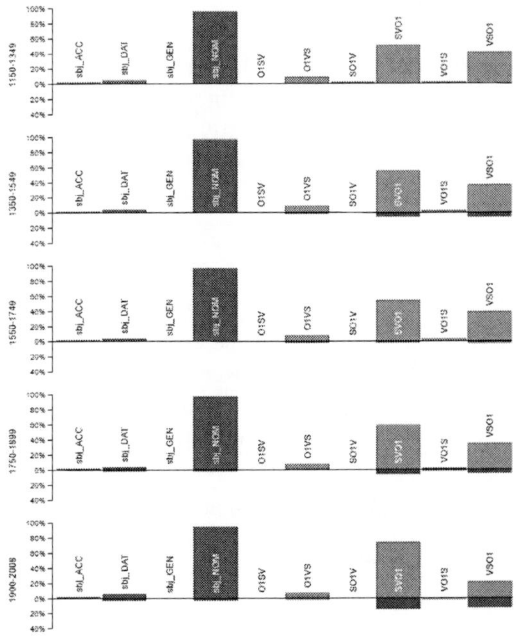

Figure 5: Word order and subject case for Range B: The blue bars represent the general distribution of subject case within the filtered data set (sentences containing a subject, a direct object and a verb). The orange bars represent the possible word order patterns occurring in the data. Over time, SVO increases consistently with respect to each previous time period (green bar). At the same time, VSO decreases (red bar). The dimension subject case remains stable until the last time period in which a slight increase of dative subjects is visible.

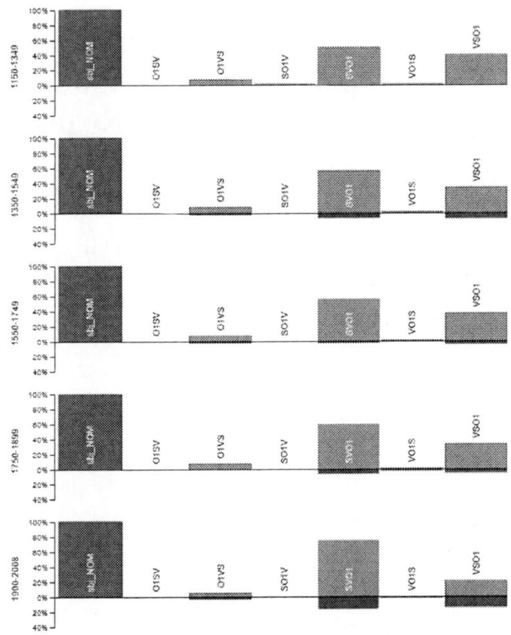

Figure 6: Word order for Range B for nominative subjects. The diachrony of the word order patterns corresponds to the one found for all subjects (as displayed in Figure 5), i.e., VSO is decreasing across the time stages, while SVO is increasing.

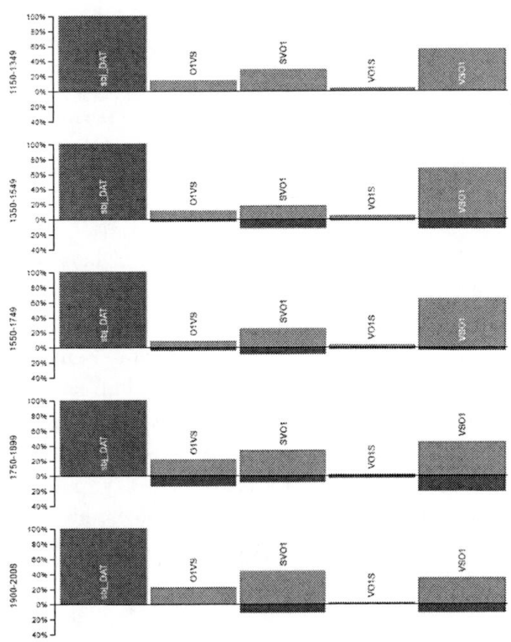

Figure 7: Word order for Range B for dative subjects. VSO is the dominant word order up until the last time stage in which SVO becomes the dominant word order after continuously increasing along the whole corpus. Moreover, OVS word order stands out in the second to last time stage.

Comparing Rule-based and SMT-based Spelling Normalisation for English Historical Texts

Gerold Schneider
Institute of
Computational Linguistics
and Department of English
University of Zurich
gschneid@ifi.uzh.ch

Eva Pettersson
Department of
Linguistics and Philology
Uppsala University
eva.pettersson
@lingfil.uu.se

Michael Percillier
Department of English
University of Mannheim
percillier@uni-mannheim.de

Abstract

To be able to use existing natural language processing tools for analysing historical text, an important preprocessing step is spelling normalisation, converting the original spelling to present-day spelling, before applying tools such as taggers and parsers. In this paper, we compare a probablistic, language-independent approach to spelling normalisation based on statistical machine translation (SMT) techniques, to a rule-based system combining dictionary lookup with rules and non-probabilistic weights. The rule-based system reaches the best accuracy, up to 94% precision at 74% recall, while the SMT system improves each tested period.

1 Introduction

Language technology for historical texts poses several challenges, as earlier stages of languages are under-resourced. But language technology is helpful both to researchers in Digital Humanities and Diachronic Linguistics. Natural Language Processing (NLP) tools are needed at all levels of processing, but spelling is a particularly obvious candidate, for at least two reasons. First, historical variants not only differ from present-day spellings. They also often lack normalisation within their period – the same word often appears with several different spellings inside the same document. Thus, even simple lexicon-based research is hampered by complex corpus queries and low recall. Second, spelling variants can affect all other subsequent processing levels – tokenisation, part-of-speech tagging and parsing. For example, frequent variants like *call'd* for *called* lead to a tokenisation error, which in turn results in wrong tagging (*call_NN d_MD*), and as a consequence parsing quality is also affected. Rayson et al. (2007), Scheible et al. (2011) and Schneider et al. (2014) report that about half of the changes induced by automatic spelling normalisation lead to improved tagging and parsing, which makes it a vital contributor to improved tagging and parsing of historical texts.

Several approaches for mapping historical variants to present-day standard spelling have been proposed. For English, on which we are going to focus in this article, VARiant Detector 2 (VARD) (Baron and Rayson, 2008) is a popular spelling normalisation tool, but there are other possible approaches. Pettersson et al. (2014) compared three statistical approaches: 1) a filtering approach, 2) a Levenshtein-distance approach, and 3) a character-based statistical machine translation (SMT) approach. These approaches were applied to five languages, and for four of these (including English), the SMT-based approach yielded the best results.

In this paper, we compare the results of applying the SMT-based spelling normalisation approach to the ARCHER corpus of historical English and American texts, to the results achieved for VARD2 on the same corpus. The comparison is interesting as the approaches are significantly different: SMT is a probablistic, language-independent approach, whereas VARD2 combines lexicon-lookup with rules and non-probabilistic weights.

2 Data and Methods

2.1 The ARCHER Corpus

As corpus of application, we use ARCHER (Biber et al., 1994), a historical corpus sampled from British and American texts from 1600-1999 and across several registers. Its current version (V 3.2) contains 3.2 million words. Since there are increasingly fewer non-standard spelling variants in later texts, we have only used texts until 1850.

The increasing scarcity of non-standard spelling also gives rise to a new research question: from which point on does spelling normalisation introduce more errors than correcting the few remaining non-standard spelling variants?

For the training phase, we have manually annotated 109 documents (about 200,000 words), stratified by 4 periods (1650-99, 1700-49, 1750-99, 1800-49), with a total of 6,975 manual normalisations. For evaluation, we have manually annotated a further 30 documents, containing 1,467 normalisations. The ARCHER corpus has been carefully sampled and aims to be genre-balanced, which provides us with a realistic real-world scenario.

A first observation that we have made is that while the amount of non-standard spelling decreases (from a mean of 315 per document in the period 1600-1649 to 24 in the period from 1800-49), the variance is very large (the standard deviation in the period 1600-1649 is 266, in the period from 1800-49 it is 52), indicating that individual styles vary considerably.

2.2 SMT

In the SMT-based approach, spelling normalisation is treated as a translation task, which could be solved using statistical machine translation (SMT) techniques. To address changes in spelling rather than the full translation of words and phrases, the translation system is trained on sequences of characters instead of word sequences.

In our experiments, we use the same settings for SMT-based spelling normalisation as presented in Pettersson et al. (2013), that is a phrase-based translation model, using Moses with all its standard components (Koehn et al., 2007), and IRSTLM for language modelling (Federico et al., 2008). For aligning the characters in the historical part of the corpus to the corresponding characters in the modern version of the corpus, the word alignment toolkit GIZA++ (Och and Ney, 2003) is applied, implementing the IBM models commonly used in SMT (Brown, 1993). The same default settings as for standard machine translation are used, with the following exceptions:

1. The system is trained on sequences of characters instead of word sequences.
2. Reordering is switched off during training, since it is unlikely that the characters are to be reordered across the whole word.
3. The maximum size of a phrase (sequence of characters) is set to 10, a setting previously shown to be successful for character-based machine translation between closely related languages (Tiedemann , 2009).

2.3 VARD2

The automatic normalisation tool VARD2 (Baron and Rayson, 2008) is a rule-based system, which can be customized to learn more rules from annotated corpora and adapt weights to them. The first version of VARD was a pure dictionary-based system. VARD2 extends this approach as follows.

First, every word that is not found in the tool's present-day English (PDE) spelling lexicon is marked as a candidate. Second, PDE variants for candidates are found and ranked, according to the following three methods:

1. the original VARD replacement dictionary
2. a variant of SoundEx, which maps phonetically similar words onto each other
3. letter replacement rules, which represent commmon patterns of spelling variation, for example interchanging *v* and *u* or dropping word-final *e*.

These rules are given a non-probabilistic confidence score, and each replacement candidate is also weighted by edit distance. When further annotated corpora are added, the replacement dictionary is extended and the weights of the three methods are optimised.

As VARD2 is a rule-based and non-probabilistic system, the question arises how it performs in comparison to state-of-the-art statistical approaches. It has been shown, for example in the domain of part-of-speech tagging (Samuelsson and Voutilainen, 1997; Loftsson, 2008), that carefully written rule-based systems can perform at the same level or better than statistical systems.

3 Results

3.1 Annotation, Inter-Annotator Agreement

For evaluating the SMT method, we used the manual annotation of ARCHER (split into 90% training and 10% evaluation) as the first evaluation method. For the evaluation of VARD2, and for comparing VARD2 to SMT, we used the manually annotated 30 documents described in Section 2.1.

When annotating the evaluation set, we noticed that while in most cases normalisation is clear, there are several reasons why inter-annotator agreement is considerably lower than 100%. Four important reasons are: first, there are cases where it is unclear if a variant is PDE or not. A good example is *thou hast* where VARD2 by default changes *hast* to *have*, although this is, in the opinion of one annotator, rather a change of morphological inflection than of spelling. Second, if dictionaries list alternative readings (e.g. British and American), should one normalise? Third, it is unclear how strict to be with hyphenation: should *sun-shine* or *bridle-way* be corrected? Fourth, particularly in the recent texts, where only every 100th or 200th word has a non-standard spelling, it is very easy to overlook variants.

A subset of our evaluation corpus, comprising 7 documents, was annotated by two of the authors. On the possible 529 normalisations, they agreed on 439, which corresponds to an inter-annotator agreement of 83%. We corrected obvious oversights and otherwise took the annotations of the author who had annotated the training set.

3.2 SMT

For the SMT-based experiments, we need to train a *translation model* and a *language model*. For the translation model, we use pairs of historical word forms mapped to their corresponding normalised spelling, to calculate the likelihood that certain sequences in the target language (i.e. the modern spelling) are translations of the sequences in the source language (i.e. the historical word forms). Such word pairs were extracted from the training part of the ARCHER corpus (as described in Section 2.1) and split into a pure training part and a tuning part (as required by the Moses system) by extracting every 10th word form to the tuning part, and the rest of the word forms to the training part. For language modeling, a monolingual target language corpus is used for modeling the probabilities that any candidate translation string would occur in the target language. For this purpose, we use the British National Corpus (BNC) of approximately 100 million words sampled to represent a wide cross-section of British English from the late 20th century (BNC, 2007). We filter hapax legomena, i.e. take all word forms that appear at least twice in the BNC. In addition, the manually normalised part of the training corpus is added to the language model, to include archaic word forms that are unlikely to occur in the BNC corpus.

Historical texts are marked by a high degree of spelling variance and spelling inconsistencies, leading to data sparseness when applying different kinds of NLP tools to the data. It is therefore interesting to explore whether adding historical data in general could improve normalisation accuracy, or if the data need to be representative of the specific time period targeted. We therefore split both the training and the evaluation parts of the ARCHER corpus into three subcorpora, containing texts from the 17th, 18th, and 19th century respectively. This way, we can evaluate normalisation accuracy for each subcorpus, when trained on data from all three centuries, and when trained on data from the specific time period only.

For the SMT-based approach, we then ran experiments by 1) training on the full corpus of manually normalised historical text, 2) training on the correct century only (17th, 18th or 19th), and 3) adding dictionaries in two ways:

(a) Historical word forms that are found in the manually normalised part of the training corpus are left unchanged.

(b) A normalisation candidate suggested by the SMT system is only accepted if it occurs in the BNC corpus.

Full Test Corpus	
Unnormalised	97.21
Training corpus	98.00
Training corpus + Dict (a)	98.14
Training corpus + Dict (b)	98.01
Training corpus + Dict (a) & (b)	98.14
17th Century Part of the Test Corpus	
Unnormalised	93.88
Full training corpus	96.60
17th century part of the training corpus	96.89
18th Century Part of the Test Corpus	
Unnormalised	98.65
Full training corpus	98.75
18th century part of the training corpus	98.69
19th Century Part of the Test Corpus	
Unnormalised	98.95
Full training corpus	99.10
19th century part of the training corpus	99.15

Table 1: Normalisation accuracy, per word, for different parts of the corpus. dict = adding dictionaries for lexical filtering.

As shown in Table 1, normalisation accuracy improves for all parts of the corpus, using the SMT-based approach to spelling normalisation. There are 421 cases where the SMT-based system has modified the original spelling to a spelling identical to the manually defined gold standard spelling, e.g.:

happinesse → *happiness*
onely → *only*
relligious → *religious*
iustices → *justices*
loue → *love*

In contrast, there are 44 cases where the SMT-based system has suggested a modification that is different from the gold standard spelling, i.e. precision errors. In most of these cases, the normalisation system has failed, but there are also instances that seem to be due to mistakes in the manually defined gold standard.

In 762 cases, the normalisation system has left the original word form unchanged, even though the manually defined gold standard suggest a normalisation, i.e.we have a recall error. A manual error analysis shows that one of the major cause of recall errors involves apostrophes, e.g.:

mans ↛ *man's*
o'er ↛ *over*
redeem'd ↛ *redeemed*
y'are ↛ *you're*

Other common causes of recall error are connected to endings like *-ie*, *-y*, *e* and *eth*, e.g.:

flie ↛ *fly*
easie ↛ *easy*
disdaine ↛ *disdain*
gipsey ↛ *gypsy*
captaine ↛ *captain*
seemeth ↛ *seems*

Furthermore, using the manually normalised part of the training data as a filter, leaving word forms that occur in this data set unnormalised, has a positive effect on normalisation accuracy. The main reason is the otherwise incorrect normalisation of frequently occurring function words, such as *thy* and *thee*. In the manual normalisation process, these word forms have been left as they are. The SMT-based system would however, without lexical filtering, normalise these word forms into *they* and *the* respectively, due to the strong preference for these word forms in the language model. Even though the manually normalised version of the ARCHER training data, including word forms such as *thy* and *thee*, have been added to the language model, these occurrences are outnumbered by the occurrences of the much more frequent English word forms *the* and *they* in the BNC part of the language model.

The second lexical filtering, where normalisation candidates suggested by the SMT system are only accepted if occurring in the BNC corpus, also leads to a small (non-significant) improvement of the normalisation accuracy. The results presented for the time-specific subcorpora are thus based on lexical filtering using both methods.

It is interesting to note that for both 17th century data and 19th century data, the best normalisation accuracy is achieved if a smaller data set containing time-specific data only is used, rather than adding training data from all three centuries.

3.3 VARD2 Performance on Evaluation Set

The results of applying VARD2 are given in Table 2, in terms of precison, recall, and per-word rates. The results using the default rules provided with the VARD2 distribution are in the second column, and using the training from the manually annotated 109 ARCHER documents (in addition to the default rules provided in the VARD2 distribution) in the third column, and best SMT in the fourth column.

Table 2 shows five points. First, VARD2 improves spelling (in the sense of mapping it to PDE variants) in most settings, except when applying the defaults settings to the latest period, 19th century texts.

Second, the training with ARCHER has considerably improved results.

Third, we have tested the effect of training on the entire ARCHER or only the appropriate century and show the results in the second last column. The effect of training VARD2 on different periods could be relatively small, as the default rules are not deleted, the new rules are just added and the the weights adapted. Using less training data leads to results with higher precision and lower recall.

Fourth, the task gets increasingly difficult in later periods, which is related to the fact that only very few tokens need normalisation, as we have already observed in the discussion of inter-annotator agreement. The performance in the 19th century is partly so low because there are only very few words that require correction, thus absurd cor-

	VARD Default	+ trained on ALL ARCHER	+ trained on ARCHER ct.	best SMT
Full Evaluation Corpus (N=838,W=29167)				
Precision	89.54	94.36	–	80.48
Recall	76.61	73.89	–	64.43
Unnorm. words	97.13	97.13	–	97.13
Correct words	99.07	99.11	–	98.53
17th Century Part of the Evaluation Corpus (N=507,W=9682)				
Precision	88.31	94.81	99.43	78.93
Recall	74.56	72.00	69.42	67.26
Unnorm. words	94.76	94.76	94.76	94.76
Correct words	98.15	98.33	98.38	97.34
18th Century Part of the Evaluation Corpus (N=92,W=11478)				
Precision	83.75	92.42	100.00	78.31
Recall	72.82	66.30	65.22	70.65
Unnorm. words	99.20	99.20	99.20	99.20
Correct words	99.67	99.69	99.72	99.61
19th Century Part of the Evaluation Corpus (N=61,W=9617)				
Precision	90.63	87.23	100.00	60.71
Recall	47.54	67.21	24.59	27.87
Unnorm. words	99.36	99.36	99.36	99.36
Correct words	99.64	99.73	99.52	99.42

Table 2: Normalisation accuracy of VARD, in percent, for the evaluation corpus, and split by century, comparing the VARD default rules, and the effect of training on 109 manually annotated ARCHER documents, and a comparison to SMT. N=number of manual changes, W=number of words

rections such as changing *idiotism* to *idiocy* affect precision. Recall is strongly affected by rare words and rare but correct variants, such as *silicious* which is not corrected to *siliceous*. It might be advisable to stop using historical spelling correction already at 1800 instead of 1850.

Fifth, the SMT system performs slightly below the highly costumized VARD tool. We elaborate on this point in the following section.

4 VARD2 and SMT in comparison

Among the items that VARD2 failed to detect, hyphenation stood out in particular (e.g. *sun-shine* which should be changed to *sunshine*). On the other hand, it overgeneralizes from 2nd person singular verb forms to plural forms (e.g. *hast* and *darest* are changed to *have* and *dare*). As these are frequent forms, they have a substantial numerical impact. VARD2 also overnormalises proper names (e.g. *ALONZO* to *ALONSO*), which often keep histoical spellings in PDE. The detection of proper names in historical texts is far from trivial, however, as also common nouns and verbs are often capitalised.

When inspecting the errors made by the SMT system, we have observed the following types of errors:

- Overgeneralisation, e.g.: *whether* has incorrectly been suggested to be normalised to *wheather*.
- Undergeneralisations, e.g.: *complements* is not normalised to *compliments*, because the word *complements* also exists, with a different meaning.
- Foreign words: for example, the Latin word *mater* is incorrectly normalised to *matter*
- Inter-annotator questions, e.g.: *hath* is normalised to *have*, *insomuch* to *inasmuch*, *emphatical* to *emphatic*
- Oversights, spurious errors: Some of the suggested normalisations are correct, even though classified as incorrect when compared to the gold standard.

5 Related Work

Apart from the SMT-based approach to spelling normalisation originally described in Pettersson et al. (2013), and applied to the ARCHER corpus in this study, character-based SMT-techniques have also been implemented by Scherrer and Erjavec (2013), for the task of normalising historical Slovene. They tried both a supervised and an unsupervised learning approach. In the supervised setting, the translation model was trained on a set of 45,810 historical-modern Slovene word pairs, whereas the language model was trained on the same data set but only including the modern word forms. In addition, a lexicon filter was used, in which normalisation candidates proposed by the translation model were only accepted if they were also found in the Modern Slovene Sloleks dictionary. In the unsupervised setting, the historical-to-modern training data was created inbased on separate lists of historical word forms and modern word forms, where the historical word forms were mapped to modern word forms based on string similarity comparisons between the word forms occurring in the two lists. Their evaluation showed an increase in normalisation accuracy from 15.4% to 48.9% for 18th century test data using the unsupervised setting. In the supervised setting, accuracy improved further to 72.4%.

6 Conclusions and Outlook

We have compared a probablistic, language-independent approach to spelling normalisation based on SMT, to a carefully crafted and highly adapted rule-based system. The latter has slightly higher performance (up to 94% precision at 74% recall) while the former is more general and fully language-independent. We have tested various settings, and shown that training with smaller century-specific data sets performs better, and that statistical SMT can be improved in several ways, e.g. by constraining the dictionary to forms seen in present-day spelling.

As future work, we would like to assess the results of succeeding NLP tasks, such as tagging and parsing, based on normalised data. We will also try to improve normalisation results further by combining the two approaches in various ways. One way would be to add automatically normalised word forms using VARD to the training data for the SMT-based system. This would be considered a semi-supervised method, in which both manually revised and automatically annotated data are used for training the SMT-based system. Another way of combining the two systems would be to use the normalisations suggested by the SMT-based system to guide the VARD system in the ranking process, in cases where several normalisation candidates are given in VARD.

Many of the remaining errors are hard to correct with purely word-based approaches. We would like to investigate if using limited context can improve results.

References

Alistair Baron and Paul Rayson. 2008. VARD 2: A tool for dealing with spelling variation in historical corpora. In *Proceedings of the Postgraduate Conference in Corpus Linguistics*, Birmingham. Aston University.

Douglas Biber, Edward Finegan, and Dwight Atkinson. 1994. Archer and its challenges: Compiling and exploring a representative corpus of historical english registers. In Udo Fries, Peter Schneider, and Gunnel Tottie, editors, *Creating and using English language corpora, Papers from the 14th International Conference on English Language Research on Computerized Corpora, Zurich 1993*, pages 1–13. Rodopi, Amsterdam.

BNC Consortium. 2007. The British National Corpus, Version 3. Distributed by Oxford University Computing Services on behalf of the BNC Consortium. http://www.natcorp.ox.ac.uk/.

Peter Brown, Vincent Della Pietra, Stephen Della Pietra, and Robert Mercer. 1993. The Mathematics of Statistical Machine Translation: Parameter Estimation. *Computational Linguistics*, 19(2), pages 263–311.

Marcello Federico, Nicola Bertoldi, and Mauro Cettolo. 2008. IRSTLM: an open source toolkit for handling large scale language models. in *Proceedings of Interspeech 2008*, pages 1618–1621.

Philipp Koehn, Hieu Hoang, Alexandra Birch, Chris Callison-Burch, Marcello Federico, Nicola Bertoldi, Brooke Cowan, Wade Shen, Christine Moran, Richard Zens, Chris Dyer, Ondřej Bojar, Alexandra Constantin, and Evan Herbst, 2007. Moses: Open Source Toolkit for Statistical Machine Translation. in *Proceedings of the 45th Annual Meeting of the ACL on Interactive Poster and Demonstration Sessions*, pages 177–180.

Hrafn Loftsson. 2008. Tagging icelandic text: A linguistic rule-based approach. *Nordic Journal of Linguistics*, 31(1).

Franz Josef Och and Hermann Ney. 2003. A Systematic Comparison of Various Statistical Alignment

Models. *Computational Linguistics*, 1(29), pages 19–51.

Eva Pettersson, Beáta Megyesi, and Jörg Tiedemann. 2013. An SMT approach to automatic annotation of historical text. In *Proceedings of the NoDaLiDa 2013 workshop on Computational Historical Linguistics*.

Eva Pettersson, Beáta Megyesi, and Joakim Nivre. 2014. A multilingual evaluation of three spelling normalisation methods for historical text. In *Proceedings of the 8th Workshop on Language Technology for Cultural Heritage, Social Sciences, and Humanities (LaTeCH) @ EACL 2014*, pages 32–41, Gothenburg, Sweden.

Paul Rayson, Dawn Archer, Alistair Baron, Jonathan Culpeper, and Nicholas Smith. 2007. Tagging the bard: Evaluating the accuracy of a modern POS tagger on Early Modern English corpora. In *Proceedings of Corpus Linguistics 2007*. University of Birmingham, UK.

Silke Scheible, Richard J. Whitt, Martin Durrell, and Paul Bennett. 2011. Evaluating an 'off-the-shelf' POS-tagger on Early Modern German text. In *Proceedings of the ACL-HLT 2011 Workshop on Language Technology for Cultural Heritage, Social Sciences, and Humanities (LaTeCH 2011)*, Portland, Oregon.

Christer Samuelsson and Atro Voutilainen. 1997. Comparing a linguistic and a stochastic tagger. In *Proceedings of of ACL/EACL Joint Conference*, Madrid.

Yves Scherrer and Tomaž Erjavec. 2013. Modernizing historical Slovene words with character-based SMT. In *Proceedings of the 4th Biennial Workshop on Balto-Slavic Natural Language Processing*, pages 58–62.

Gerold Schneider, Hans Martin Lehmann, and Peter Schneider. 2014. Parsing Early Modern English corpora. *Literary and Linguistic Computing*, first published online February 6, 2014 `doi:10.1093/llc/fqu001`.

Jörg Tiedemann. 2009. Character-based PSMT for closely related languages. *Proceedings of 13th Annual Conference of the European Association for Machine Translation (EAMT'09)*, pages 12–19.

Data-driven Morphology and Sociolinguistics for Early Modern Dutch

Marijn Schraagen **Marjo van Koppen**
Utrecht Institute of Linguistics OTS
Utrecht University
{m.p.schraagen,j.m.vankoppen}@uu.nl

Feike Dietz
Institute for Cultural Inquiry
Utrecht University
f.m.dietz@uu.nl

Abstract

The advent of Early Modern Dutch (starting ~1550) marked significant developments in language use in the Netherlands. Examples include the loss of the case marking system, the loss of negative particles and the introduction of new vocabulary. These developments typically lead to a lot of variation both within and between language users. Linguistics research aims to characterize and account for such variation patterns. Due to sparseness of digital resources and tools, research is still dependent on traditional, qualitative analysis. This paper describes an ongoing effort to increase the amount of tools and resources, exploring two different routes: (i) modernization of historical language and (ii) adding linguistic and sociolinguistic annotations to historical language directly. This paper discusses and compares the experimental setup, and preliminary results of these two routes and provides an outlook on the envisioned linguistic and sociolinguistic research approach.

1 Introduction

In the 16th century, the language situation in the Netherlands changed substantially. One important influence is the interest in standardization of the Dutch language (Lambrecht, 1550; de Heuiter, 1581; Spiegel, 1584; Stevin, 1586). This standardization process was combined with ongoing developments in case marking (Weerman and de Wit, 1999), negation (Hoeksema, 1997), and various other lexical and morphosyntactic phenomena (Howell, 2006). The extent to which these developments were actually adopted by language users differs between and within individual language users (Bax and Streekstra, 2003; Nobels and Rutten, 2014).

1637:	*Ende*	*het*	*gout*	*deses*	*lants*	*is*	*goet*
1888:	En	het	goud	van dit	land	is	goed

'And the gold of that land is good'

Figure 1: Example parallel Bible translation

To date, most approaches to study these phenomena have been qualitative in nature. In this paper an ongoing effort is described to enrich Early Modern text with linguistic and sociolinguistic information in a systematic way, to allow a quantitative computational linguistic approach. The paper explores two routes to develop such an approach: a modernization route and a historical annotation route. In Section 2 an approach to text modernization is outlined. Section 3 describes an automatic tagging approach with manual post-correction and metadata enrichment. Section 4 provides a comparison between these two routes.

2 Modernization

In contrast to historical Dutch, modern Dutch is a very well-resourced language for NLP applications. A translation modernization step allows to use these resources for historical texts (Tjong Kim Sang, 2016). The modernization process can benefit from the similarity between the two historically related language varieties (Koolen et al., 2006). For the development of the modernization method described in this paper, a parallel pair of Dutch Bible translations from 1637[1] and 1888[2] is used. The close parallelism of this training pair (see Figure 1) allows for efficient application of word pair extraction algorithms. The method consists of a combination of three approaches: (i) application of manual expert rewriting rules (cf.

[1] http://dbnl.nl/tekst/_sta001stat01_01/
[2] http://www.statenvertaling.net

Braun, 2002; Robertson and Willett, 1992), (ii) extraction of a translation lexicon from parallel pairs in training data (cf. Bollmann et al., 2011), and (iii) the application of the existing statistical machine translation framework Moses (Köhn et al., 2007), cf. (Pettersson et al., 2013; Scherrer and Erjavec, 2016). In the remainder of this paper the combination of the first two approaches is referred to as the *custom method*, while the third approach is called the *SMT method*.

The dataset is split into a training part (32,235 lines, 946,721 words, 87%) and a test part (5,000 lines, 140,812 words, 13%). The split is linear, with the training part ranging from Genesis to the (apocryphic) Book of Ezra, and the test part ranging from Ezra to 3 Maccabees. For the SMT method, a subset of 2000 lines (58,249 words) is removed from the end of the training set to be used as a development set for MERT.

In Table 1 the results of the modernization approach are listed. To compare translations, the BLEU measure is used (Papineni et al., 2002). This score has notable shortcomings as a measure of translation accuracy (Callison-Burch et al., 2006), pertaining to phrase permutation and semantic unawareness. However, these shortcomings appear to be less severe for a modernization task, where phrase-based translations and word reordering are less likely to occur. Moreover, a correct translation is not the main goal of this method. Instead, the modernization is intended to increase accuracy of NLP methods, e.g., POS tagging, syntactic parsing, frequency counts, lexicon lookup, etc. It is not yet clear how well the BLEU score correlates with accuracy of these methods, however some correlation is to be expected.

The details of the custom method are as follows: as sub-baseline, **no translation** is performed. As **baseline** all parallel sentences of equal length have been extracted from the training data, and all words with an unambiguous (i.e., always the same) translation are used as a translation lexicon for the test data. Next, all sentences are **aligned** on word level to extract additional translation pairs. Note that the baseline and the alignment are relatively efficient, due to the close parallelism of the source data. Then, manual modernization **rules** are applied, specifically targeted to Early Modern Dutch, such as case marker normalization, negation normalization, clitic separation, numeral normalization. Note that phonetic rewriting is not part of this step. Next, translation pairs are constructed for **multiple word** translations (e.g., *deses* $\rightarrow$ *van dit* in Figure 1, English: this$_{\text{GEN}}$ $\rightarrow$ of this). At this point, the test set is already sufficiently modern to allow accurate POS tagging, at least on the tokens that have been assigned the correct, modern translation. This **POS information** can be used to translate a historical word in different ways conditional on the surrounding POS tags. This is similar to the multiple word translation, except that the selection on POS tags allows to generalize over the vocabulary. As an example, the pronoun *haer* is likely to be translated as *hen* (them) before a verb, and as *hun* (their) before a noun. To limit sparseness issues, the main POS tag is used without features. For both the multiple word and the POS step, pairs have been selected using hill-climbing, implemented as incremental inclusion of those pairs that increase the BLEU score on the training set. Note that, since the pairs are extracted from the training set (i.e., a development set is not used), the hill-climbing selection is equivalent to selecting translations with a true positive application rate of over 0.5. Finally, a number of highly document-specific rules have been applied to address differences in **punctuation** between the two Bible translations. Examples of rules and word pairs are provided in Table 2.

For the evaluation of the SMT method, a different sequence of steps is applied. First, a model is built by Moses using the training set with **basic** settings. Then, **MERT tuning** is applied using the development set. Next, the **capitalization** model of Moses, which turned out to be highly inaccu-

method	*steps*	BLEU
custom	no translation	0.134
	baseline	0.507
	aligned	0.530
	rules	0.581
	multiple word	0.600
	POS information	0.619
	punctuation	0.627
SMT	Moses basic	0.597
	MERT tuning	0.616
	capitalization	0.639
combination	rules	0.644
	multiple word, POS	0.647
	punctuation	0.653

Table 1: Translation evaluation

input	output	notes	translation
	rewriting rules		
stem+se	*stem* ␣ hen	pronoun clisis	them
eens *stems*	van een	genitive	of a
den/mijnen/welken	de/mijn/welke	case loss	the/mine/which
alle de	al de	agreement loss	all the
en [. . .] *negative*	*negative*	negative concord	
numeral ␣ ende ␣ *num*	*num*+en+*num*		
num ␣ *num*	*num*+*num*		
	punctuation rules		
`␣	␣		
; *[upper case]*	:		
; *[lower case]*	,		
said, *[upper case]*	:		
	extracted multiword pairs		
haer zelfden	zichzelf	reflexive pronoun	him/her/it/them/oneself
waer heen	waarheen	prepositional compound	where to
leeuws tanden	leeuwentanden	case loss, compounding	lion teeth
potte-backers kruik	pottenbakkerskruik	case loss, compounding	pottery jar
rechteroog heupe	rechterheup	terminology shift	right hand side hip
	extracted Part-of-Speech pairs		
alle+V	allen		all
alle+PRON	al		all
PUNCT+alle	al		all
daar+V	er		there

Table 2: Example implementations of translation steps

rate, is corrected using post-processing. Combining the SMT and the custom method, manual rewriting **rules** are applied on top of SMT, followed by **multiple word** alignment, **POS** information and **punctuation rules**.

2.1 Discussion

Both the method using manual rules combined with automatic translation pair extraction as well as the method using the Moses toolkit show a substantial improvement over the baseline performance. For the first method, the manual rule component provides the largest share of the performance improvement. This indicates (consistent with, e.g., Pettersson et al., 2012) that language development over time, at least in the case of Bible translations, displays a high level of regularity, which can be captured by a small number of rewriting rules. Interestingly, the morphological rules combined with translation pair extraction offer sufficient coverage to omit phonetic rewriting commonly used in language modernization. Note that this behavior depends on similarity between training and test vocabulary, which will be discussed further in Section 2.1.1.

The described method provides competitive performance as compared to the SMT approach. It can be considered promising that the results of a state-of-the-art machine learning algorithm can be reproduced using a relatively straightforward approach. However, Table 1 also shows that the combination of approaches offers very little improvement over the performance of the SMT algorithm in isolation. Therefore, it is at present not fully clear how to incorporate the custom translation pair extraction or manual morphological rules into a combined methodology.

To obtain a better insight in the performance of the various methods, a more extensive evaluation is necessary. This includes the application of the method on more diverse data and a systematic comparison between approaches. Furthermore, the evaluation could be extended into a more application–oriented direction, i.e., by analyzing results of NLP methods on modernized text.

2.1.1 CLIN27 Shared Task

The method presented in this paper has also been entered into the CLIN27 Shared Task on Translating Historical Text[3]. The results of the system on this task are considerably lower than in the present evaluation, which can be contributed to several factors.

First, the test set used for the Shared Task was markedly different from the provided training set. The test set contained genres such as theater plays, letters, eulogies, administrative texts, journal entries, and bullet point lists of activities. These genres introduce a significant amount of new vocabulary, for which the word-level vocabulary-based method as presented in this paper is not particularly well-suited. In the Shared Task the method was extended with a set of phonetic rewriting rules, which showed a large performance increase. This is consistent with previous work on character-level SMT approaches (e.g., Scherrer and Erjavec, 2013), which are essentially a way to automatically extract phonetic rewriting rules from data.

Furthermore, the test set contained texts ranging from 1607 to 1692. Various morphosyntactic or spelling-related phenomena occurring in the 1637 training set which are targeted with specific rules do not occur in later texts, such as negative concord constructions. Application of these rules on later texts actually decreases performance in certain cases, and should therefore be controlled by time period constraints.

Additionally, the test set fot the Shared Task was created with the specific goal of word-level spelling modernization to facilitate POS tagging (cf. Tjong Kim Sang, 2016). This resulted in a rather artificial translation, preserving sentence length and word order, leaving historical word forms untranslated in case a modern tagger already assigned a correct tag. As a result, in several cases the current method provides an arguably better translation which is nevertheless evaluated as an error. Further analysis showed that, for a number of participants in the Shared Task, manually re-spelling a very small number of frequent errors resulted in a substantial performance improvement.

For the reasons mentioned above, the results on the CLIN27 Shared Task should not be considered as a conclusive evaluation of the current method. However, the results do indicate important aspects of the current method, such as the impact of training vocabulary, and the influence of the goal application on the translation requirements. Further development of these issues is ongoing in the current project.

[3] https://ifarm.nl/clin2017st/

3 Annotation

As stated above, text modernization allows for the use of resources and tools for contemporary language. However, this approach also introduces incorrectly translated and non-translated tokens, which limit the accuracy of NLP applications. Moreover, certain information from the historical text is lost. Modernization entails spelling normalization, which means that, e.g., spelling differences over time can no longer be studied. Other topics of research, such as case marking or negation, may also be lost after modernization, or it may prove difficult to link the modernized text to the historical original. Therefore, an additional research direction processes historical text directly, using tools and resources for historical language or using manual annotation. The annotation effort also allows extension to sociolinguistic information, which is intrinsically outside the scope of modernization approaches. The remainder of this section describes the setup of the annotation task, which are currently ongoing.

3.1 Part-of-speech tagging

A pilot project has been designed to annotate a corpus of letters by the Dutch author and politician P.C. Hooft, written between 1600 and 1647. In the absence of tools for Early Modern Dutch, a POS tagger for Middle Dutch (1200–1500) is used (van Halteren and Rem, 2013). Although Middle Dutch is considerably different from Early Modern Dutch, several properties of interest are shared, such as case marking and negation clitics. Therefore, a tagger capable of marking such properties is preferred over contemporary equivalents. However, as expected on Early Modern data, the overall accuracy of the tagger is low. Therefore, a manual annotation effort is ongoing to check and correct all assigned tags (including morphosyntactic features) in the corpus manually.

3.2 Sociolinguistic tagging

An accurately tagged corpus allows to discover patterns on a morphosyntactic level. To analyze the development of such phenomena, non-linguistic variables have to be taken into account.

Als	*nu*	*de*	*veerschujt*	*niet*	*anders*	*ujt*	***en***	*leverde*	*dan*	*den*	*brief*
Con(sub)	Adv(gen)	Det()	N(sg)	Pro(neg)	Adj(-s)	Adp(prtcl)	**Adj(negcl)**	V(past)	Con(cmp)	Det(-n)	N(sg)
If	now	the	ferry	nothing	else	out	**not**	delivered	than	the	letter

'If the ferry would not deliver anything but the letter'

Figure 2: Example tagged sentence, showing a negation clitic

The letter corpus contains dated documents, therefore a straighforward variable is time, allowing analysis of when certain developments have occurred. Other variables of interest include the topic of correspondence, the type of relation between the correspondents and the domain of the correspondence (government, finance, literature, etc.), the goal of the correspondence (invitation, recommendation, request, etc.), and personal information about the correspondent (age, gender, literary status). Furthermore, the rhetorical structure of a text is annotated, in terms of greeting, opening, body, closing. This for instance allows to verify the hypothesis that certain parts of letters, e.g., the opening and closing sections, are highly formulaic, and therefore do not exhibit language development to the same degree as the body text (Nobels and Rutten, 2014). Annotation is performed by a pool of nine annotators. To measure inter-annotator agreement, 10% of the corpus is assigned to random pairs of annotators. The full list of sociolinguistic variables is provided in the Appendix.

In Figure 2 an example sentence with part-of-speech tags is provided. This sentence contains the negation clitic *en*, alongside the main negation *niet*. Once the full corpus is properly tagged this clitic can be studied systematically, e.g., to investigate the neighbouring tags or lemmas of the clitic, or to check whether or not the clitic is used more often in formal writing.

3.3 Interoperability

To increase the practical accessibility of the annotation data, a collaboration with the Nederlab project (Brugman et al., 2016) has been established. Nederlab provides an online search interface for the data in the Digital Library of Dutch Literature[4] using Corpus Query Processor (Evert and Hardie, 2011), which allows to search for linguistic annotation and metadata. For this collaboration, several interoperability issues need to be addressed. The Adelheid tagger uses the CRM tagset, which contains a set of features specific for Middle Dutch. The Nederlab project uses the CGN tagset (van Eynde et al., 2000), for which both the main tags and the feature set differ considerably from CRM. For the current pilot several additional features are introduced to facilitate the analysis of language development.

Apart from the tagset, the output format needs to be converted as well. Nederlab uses the FoLiA format (van Gompel and Reynaert, 2013), which is a de facto standard XML linguistic annotation format for Dutch, whereas Adelheid uses a custom XML format. To facilitate integration with current annotations and metadata in Nederlab, a word-level alignment of the FoliA output is planned.

Further interoperability considerations include incorporation of linked data, e.g., for correspondents in the current dataset which may also be found in encyclopedic resources, and using existing classification schemes, such as HISCO for historical occupational titles (van Leeuwen et al., 2002).

4 Data-driven historical linguistics

The two methods outlined in this paper are intended to complement eachother in providing an environment for computational historical linguistics research. Modernization has the advantage that research questions can be addressed using the existing infrastructure for a modern language, in terms of resources, approaches, evaluation data et cetera. The disadvantage of this method is the inherent loss of information and the occurence of translation errors, which entails that several topics of interest cannot be studied using modernized data, or that the validity of results is unclear. In contrast, manual enrichment provides high-quality linguistic annotations as well as the possibility to include meta-linguistic information. The obvious disadvantage of this method is the large amount of time and/or financial resources necessary. However, if a sufficiently large amount of data is an-

[4] `http://www.dbnl.org`, in Dutch

notated (possibly in combination with automatically derived annotations, cf. Hupkes and Bod, 2016), machine learning algorithms can be trained to allow for automatic annotation. The combination of modernization and manual annotation may prove valuable as a methodology in historical (socio-)linguistics. Future work in the current project, however, is necessary to validate this claim.

References

Marcel Bax and Nanne Streekstra. 2003. Civil rites: ritual politeness in early modern Dutch letter–writing. *Journal of Historical Pragmatics*, 4(2):303–325.

Marcel Bollmann, Florian Petran, and Stefanie Dipper. 2011. Rule-based normalization of historical texts. In *Proceedings of Language Technologies for Digital Humanities and Cultural Heritage Workshop*, pages 34–42. ACL.

Loes Braun. 2002. Information retrieval from Dutch historical corpora. Master's thesis, Maastricht University.

Hennie Brugman, Martin Reynaert, Nicoline van der Sijs, René van Stipriaan, Erik Tjong Kim Sang, and Antal van den Bosch. 2016. Nederlab: Towards a single portal and research environment for diachronic Dutch text corpora. In *Proceedings of LREC 2016*.

Chris Callison-Burch, Miles Osborne, and Philipp Köhn. 2006. Re-evaluation the role of BLEU in machine translation research. In *Proceedings of EACL*, pages 249–256. ACL.

Stefan Evert and Andrew Hardie. 2011. Twenty-first century corpus workbench: Updating a query architecture for the new millennium. In *Proceedings of the Corpus Linguistics 2011 conference*. University of Birmingham.

Frank van Eynde, Jakub Zavrel, and Walter Daelemans. 2000. Part of speech tagging and lemmatisation for the Spoken Dutch Corpus. In *Proceedings of LREC 2000*.

Maarten van Gompel and Martin Reynaert. 2013. FoLiA: A practical XML format for linguistic annotation-a descriptive and comparative study. *Computational Linguistics in the Netherlands Journal*, 3:63–81.

Hans van Halteren and Margit Rem. 2013. Dealing with orthographic variation in a tagger-lemmatizer for fourteenth century Dutch charters. *Language Resources and Evaluation*, 47(4):1233–1259.

Pontus de Heuiter. 1581. *Nederduitse orthographie*. Edited by G.R.W. Dibbets, 1972, Wolters-Noordhoff.

Jack Hoeksema. 1997. Negation and negative concord in Middle Dutch. *Amsterdam Studies in the Theory and History of Linguistic Science*, 4:139–156.

Robert Howell. 2006. Immigration and koineisation: the formation of Early Modern Dutch urban vernaculars. *Transactions of the Philological Society*, 104(2):207–227.

Dieuwke Hupkes and Rens Bod. 2016. Pos-tagging of historical Dutch. In *Proceedings of LREC 2016*.

Philipp Köhn, Hieu Hoang, Alexandra Birch, et al. 2007. Moses: Open source toolkit for statistical machine translation. In *Proceedings of the 45th annual meeting of the ACL on interactive poster and demonstration sessions*, pages 177–180. Association for Computational Linguistics.

Marijn Koolen, Frans Adriaans, Jaap Kamps, and Maarten de Rijke. 2006. A cross-language approach to historic document retrieval. In *ECIR 2006: Proceedings of the 28th European Conference on IR Research*, pages 407–419. Springer.

Joos Lambrecht. 1550. *Nederlandsche spellijnghe, uutghesteld by vraghe ende antwoorde*. Edited by J.F.J. Heremans and F. Vanderhaeghen, 1882, C. Annoot-Braeckman.

Marco van Leeuwen, Ineke Maas, and Andrew Miles. 2002. *HISCO: Historical International Standard Classification of Occupations*. Cornell University Press.

Judith Nobels and Gijsbert Rutten. 2014. Language norms and language use in seventeenth-century Dutch: negation and the genitive. In Gijsbert Rutten, editor, *Norms and usage in language history, 1600-1900. A sociolinguistic and comparative perspective.*, pages 21–48. John Benjamins Publishing Company.

Kishore Papineni, Salim Roukos, Todd Ward, and Wei-Jing Zhu. 2002. BLEU: a method for automatic evaluation of machine translation. In *Proceedings of the 40th annual meeting on association for computational linguistics*, pages 311–318. Association for Computational Linguistics.

Eva Pettersson, Beáta Megyesi, and Joakim Nivre. 2012. Rule-based normalisation of historical text - a diachronic study. In *Proceedings of the First international Workshop on Language Technology for Historical Text*, KONVENS, pages 333–341.

Eva Pettersson, Beáta Megyesi, and Jörg Tiedemann. 2013. An SMT approach to automatic annotation of historical text. In *Proceedings of the workshop on computational historical linguistics at NODALIDA*, pages 54–69. Linköping.

Alexander Robertson and Peter Willett. 1992. Searching for historical word-forms in a database of 17th-century English text using spelling-correction methods. In *Proceedings of ACM SIGIR '92*, pages 256–265. ACM.

Yves Scherrer and Tomaž Erjavec. 2013. Modernizing historical Slovene words with character-based SMT. In *BSNLP 2013-4th Biennial Workshop on Balto-Slavic Natural Language Processing*.

Yves Scherrer and Tomaž Erjavec. 2016. Modernising historical slovene words. *Natural Language Engineering*, 22(6):881–905.

Hendrik Spiegel. 1584. *Twe-spraack. Ruygh-bewerp. Kort begrip. Rederijck-kunst.* Edited by W.J.H. Caron, 1962, Wolters-Noordhoff.

Simon Stevin. 1586. *Uytspraeck van de weerdicheyt der Duytsche tael.* Chr. Plantijn.

Erik Tjong Kim Sang. 2016. Improving part-of-speech tagging of historical text by first translating to modern text. In *Proceedings of the International Workshop on Computational History and Data-Driven Humanities*, pages 54–64. Springer.

Fred Weerman and Petra de Wit. 1999. The decline of the genitive in Dutch. *Linguistics*, 37(6):1155–1192.

Appendix: sociolinguistic variables

- Purpose of the letter
  - Express thanks
  - Compliment/praise
  - Excuse
  - Ask for a favour
  - Ask for information
  - Ask for advice
  - Admonish
  - Inform
  - Remember
  - Persuade
  - Order
  - Allow
  - Invite
- Topic of the letter
  - Business
  - Literature
  - Domestic affairs
  - Love
  - Death
  - News
  - Religion/ethics
- Correspondent information
  - name
  - group or individual
    for individuals:
  - birth/death date
  - gender
  - occupation
  - literary author
  - relation to P.C. Hooft
- Letter structure
  - Introductory greeting
  - Opening (optional)
  - Narratio
  - Closing (optional)
  - Final greeting

Applying BLAST to Text Reuse Detection in Finnish Newspapers and Journals, 1771–1910

Aleksi Vesanto
Turku NLP Group
Department of FT
University of Turku
aleksi.vesanto@utu.fi

Asko Nivala
Cultural History and
Turku Institute for Advanced Studies
University of Turku
asko.nivala@utu.fi

Heli Rantala
Cultural History
University of Turku
heli.rantala@utu.fi

Tapio Salakoski
Turku NLP Group
Department of FT
University of Turku
tapio.salakoski@utu.fi

Hannu Salmi
Cultural History
University of Turku
hannu.salmi@utu.fi

Filip Ginter
Turku NLP Group
Department of FT
University of Turku
filip.ginter@utu.fi

Abstract

We present the results of text reuse detection, based on the corpus of scanned and OCR-recognized Finnish newspapers and journals from 1771 to 1910. Our study draws on BLAST, a software created for comparing and aligning biological sequences. We show different types of text reuse in this corpus, and also present a comparison to the software Passim, developed at the Northeastern University in Boston, for text reuse detection.

1 Introduction

The dataset of the National Library of Finland (NLF) contains 1.95 million pages of digitized historical newspapers and journals from 1771 to 1910. Approximately half of the content is in Swedish, the other half in Finnish, although there are also a few German and Russian papers included (Pääkkönen et al., 2016). We aim to trace the influential texts that were copied and recirculated in Finnish newspapers and journals in this time period. This is done by clustering the 1771–1910 NLF corpus with a text reuse detection algorithm. Our approach enables us to study the dissemination of news and other information and to reconstruct the development of the newspaper network as a part of Finnish public discourse: What kinds of texts were widely shared? How fast did they spread and what were the most important nodes in the Finnish media network?

Our research project builds on a similar study of nineteenth-century US newspapers by Ryan Cordell, David A. Smith and their research group (Cordell, 2015; Smith et al., 2015). However, in contrast to the US press, the nineteenth- and early twentieth-century Finnish newspapers were typically printed in the *Fraktur* typeface, which (together with other possible sources of noise) poses unusual difficulties for Optical Character Recognition (Kettunen, 2016). To solve this problem, we have developed a novel text reuse detection solution based on BLAST (Vesanto et al., 2017) that is accurate and resistant to OCR mistakes and other noise, making the text circulation and virality of newspaper publicity in Finland a feasible research question.

2 Detecting Text Reuse

In the nineteenth century, contemporaries saw newspapers as reflections of modern culture. Many phenomena were amplified by the increasing power of the press, including urbanization, consumerism, and business life. The changes in transport technology led to more efficient distribution of information. Before 1880s, there was no copyright agreement to regulate the free copying of texts, which became a distinctive feature of the press. To understand this process, it is essential to analyze how texts were copied and reprinted.

In Finland, newspaper publishing started slowly, the first paper being *Tidningar Utgifne af et Sällskap i Åbo* in 1771. According to the NLF metadata, in 1850 there were only ten papers and six journals. A rapid upheaval occurred at the

Multta t\ä@tä fyNlkÃĎsiii kchtalostu ,ct , Äbouil Äsi ,3 wic!lä ticiun 't>t ,mitää>«, »vaalii luiftti iloista M,m<iä Tshiragauissa, Âľelä fi:föf3>i'öi että uiUfatfpäim –uhkaisiloui i Hviarat, miinto fu^tiaani 'fatifefi– fuffotai» lÃĎuja THi roinin, puutarhassa ja, ipici 'ilitsi hwi'tt<iiöii fmmiamcrk^iUi ja anoo» »imilyMla,

Mutta tästä synkästä kohtalosta ei Äbbul Äsib »ielä tiennyt mitään, vaan »ietti iloista elämää TshiraganiSsa. Sekä sis»Stä «tt ä ulkoapäin uhkasivat «aarat. mutta sulttaani katseli lukkotaisteluja Tfhiiaaanin puutarhassa ja palkitsi voittajan lunnicnnerleillä ja arÂř vonimityksillä.

Figure 1: Example of how low the OCR quality can be. Both passages are identical in the original issues.

end of the century, resulting in 89 papers and 203 journals in 1900. The volume of the press was thus very limited during the first half of the century, which also means that text reuse was small-scale. Towards the end of the period the situation changed dramatically, offering more volume for viral chains of reprints. These chains had different origins: they were internal chains within the press, translations from abroad, stories from books, telegrams, or official announcements. Therefore, text reuse detection can shed essential light on how information flowed between centers within the country and how, in the end, Finnish press participated in the global circulation of information.

The primary obstacle in detecting text reuse in the NLF dataset is the poor OCR recognition rate, as illustrated in Figure 1. This makes any approach which assumes exact seed overlaps of several words in length infeasible, and calls for a fuzzy matching method highly tolerant to noise. To this end, we have applied BLAST (Altschul et al., 1990), a sequence alignment software developed for fast matching of biological sequences against very large sequence databases. The main features of BLAST are speed and the ability to retrieve also distantly related sequences – which in our case translates to the ability to withstand the OCR noise present in the data. We index each page of the NLF data as a sequence in BLAST, translating the 23 most common lowercase letters into the amino-acid sequences which BLAST is hard-coded to handle, and subsequently matching the pages in an all-against-all scenario, and post-processing the results to recover the repeated text segments. We choose not to describe the technical details of the process in this paper, and rather focus on the results obtained. The implementation will be made available as open-source software and in the following, we focus on presenting the main results in context of processing historical texts.

System	% of text
BLAST	0.177
Passim (default)	0.057
Passim (optimized)	0.080

Table 1: Text reuse recall comparison of the BLAST-based method relative to Passim with its settings left at their default values, as well as optimized to maximize recall.

3 Text Reuse Clusters – Quantitative Analysis

In total, we found around 8 million clusters of repeated texts that have a total of 49 million occurrences (hits) longer than 300 characters. Note, however, that some clusters refer to the same, larger repeated news piece, in different lengths. This is due to the fact that at times the OCR quality is too low, allowing only for a shorter hit to be identified in some of the repetitions of an otherwise larger text. Since the surrounding text of a shorter hit is too dissimilar (which, after all, is the very reason why only a shorter segment was found), it is difficult to establish whether these clusters can be safely merged. Therefore, the number of found hits does not necessarily fully correspond to the number of unique text reuse.

3.1 BLAST evaluation

As there is not a feasible manner in which to directly estimate the recall of the system on this data, we compare our system to *Passim*, a popular tool for text reuse detection (Smith et al., 2014) used in many similar studies previously, so as to establish a relative comparison to the state-of-the-art. We form a dataset of 2,000 randomly selected documents from the NLF corpus, apply both systems to it, and for every document, we calculate the fraction of its text that was identified as text reuse, with a text length minimum set to 100. The results are summarized in Table 1, and demonstrate a substantial recall gain of the BLAST-based method.

We can see that the BLAST-based method

vastly outperforms Passim in terms of recall. In order to establish that this gain in recall is not at the expense of precision, we sample clusters both randomly and at the very bottom of BLAST similarity scores still acceptable for inclusion in the results and manually verify the proportion of those that are true positives. The proportions are shown in Table 2. The results naturally depend on the length of the texts in the cluster, with shorter texts less likely to be correct hits than the longer ones, given a constant alignment score.

Range	BLAST			Passim
	Precision random	Precision low	Coverage	Coverage
300 - 350	1.00	1.00	0.108	0.076
250 - 299	1.00	0.94	0.120	0.078
200 - 249	0.94	0.94	0.133	0.079
150 - 199	0.92	0.86	0.154	0.080
100 - 149	0.86	0.70	0.177	0.080

Table 2: The precision and coverage of the BLAST method on 50 clusters of varying text hit lengths, sampled randomly and at the lowest alignment scores acceptable.

To understand to what extent the hits identified as text re-use are dissimilar, we randomly selected 1000 clusters which contain only two hits of at least 300 characters in length. We then calculate the pairwise character alignment between these two hits and measure the proportion of matching characters, i.e. not gaps nor misalignments. As shown in Figure 2, the alignment values range from around 99% down to as low as 40%, with the bulk of the data in the 70–90% range. For the most part, the repeated texts thus differ in 10–30% of positions, but the difference can be as much as 60%. Partly, these are cases of e.g. advertisements which differ only in numerical values, but partly these are in fact fully identical texts with a massive OCR error rate.

The gain in recall comes at the expense of compute time, with BLAST being about three orders of magnitude slower than Passim. Applying BLAST to the entire NLF dataset required around 150,000 CPU-core hours. This is certainly out of reach for a single computer, but well within modern cluster computing resources, especially since the historical text collection is static and the run only needs to be carried out once.

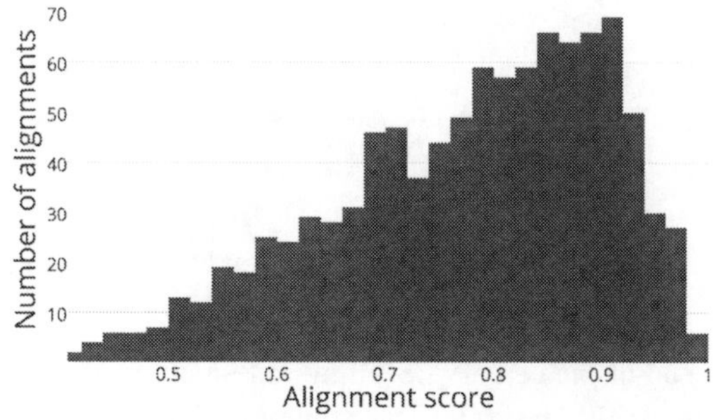

Figure 2: The distribution of alignment scores (horizontal axis) and the number of clusters out of 1000 with the given alignment score (vertical axis). Minimum text reuse length is 300.

4 Text Reuse Clusters – Qualitative Analysis

Copying and reprinting texts from other newspapers took three different forms, which is why we need to differentiate between text reuse, long-term reuse and virality. First, the majority of reprinted clusters consists of advertisements and notices, official announcements and ecclesiastical material. Second, many clusters include old news items, anecdotes, stories and poems that are suddenly reprinted many decades – sometimes even a hundred years – later. This second group is an example of longitudinal text reuse. Finally, the third group is viral news proper. The amount of viral news increases towards the end of the nineteenth century and these texts are often reprinted very rapidly within a short time frame.

4.1 Advertisements and announcements

The first group of clusters, advertisements and announcements, might be interesting sources in their own right for specific research questions. But above all, the changes in their amount tell us a lot about the scope of the public communication network and its historical development year by year even if we completely overlook the content of shared texts. For instance, by importing all text clusters as nodes and edges to a network analysis software, one is able to produce visualizations of the development of relationships between the newspapers and show what were the most dominating nodes in the network.

4.2 Longitudinal text reuse

Because of the wide time frame of the NLF dataset, long-term text reuse opens up an important perspective on historical memory. For instance, the Fennomans were an influential group in the nineteenth-century publicity of the Grand Duchy of Finland. The papers published around the turn of the nineteenth century often reprinted old articles and shorter quotations that supported their cause. To give an example of this, the Table 3 shows the reprints of a patriotic student song "Ännu på tidens mörka vågor" that was probably written by Gustaf Idestam (1802–1851) and first printed in *Åbo Morgonblad* in 3 March 1821 – a newspaper edited by the polemical Romanticist author Adolf Ivar Ardwidsson (1791–1858). The lyrics of the song were then reprinted three times in 1891, crediting the Swedish humorous magazine *Söndags-Nisse* as their source in addition to Arwidsson's paper. The song is also described in *Nya Pressen* as the favourite anthem of the Turku students before the introduction of "Vårt land", the later national anthem. We have found many other similar examples that show the way in which much earlier historical texts were reused for political purposes, opening up an important research question for the strategies of Finnish nationalism.

One example explicitly connected with the state of the Finnish press is the closing down of Arwidsson's newspaper *Åbo Morgonblad* by the officials in October 1821. The reasons for this act were political since Arwidsson had been calling for the wide freedom of the press in his paper. In the last issue of *Åbo Morgonblad* Arwidsson published the document on the official decision for the act. In 1891, 70 years later, this text was reprinted by five different newspapers. The first reprint was in *Åbo Tidningar* (30 September 1891), which used the censorship case of 1821 to discuss the state of the press freedom in 1891 – the censorship law was tightened in Autumn 1891. Other newspapers continued this discussion by reprinting the document from 1821 and also commenting the state of the censorship in 1891. This way the reuse of old news item offered a way to discuss and criticize the situation of the press freedom in 1891.

4.3 Viral news

The third group of text reuse are the actual viral news. According to our preliminary survey of the clustered NLF newspaper corpus, their amount increases rapidly after the The Crimean War (1853–1856). For instance, a bank robbery in Helsinki broke the news in 20 newspapers in 1906. This item was disseminated very rapidly in the Finnish-language press, as is shown in the Table 4. Only in six days it traveled from the urban communication hubs like Helsinki, Turku, Viipuri and Tampere to smaller towns in Ostrobothnia, Savonia, Karelia and Lapland. The viral chain served the need to rapidly tell about a current incident, although this happened without any particular plan, through the existing network of newspapers.

The three categories of text reuse could also overlap. Longitudinal chains, for example, might later on transform into viral texts. Old stories or anecdotes could be reactivated after several decades and reused in an infectious manner. BLAST is effective in revealing these different temporal rhythms of text reuse.

Cluster	Date	Title
639828	1821-03-03	Åbo Morgonblad
639828	1891-02-20	Nya Pressen
639828	1891-02-20	Folkwännen
639828	1891-02-21	Åbo Tidning

Table 3: Reprints of a patriotic song.

Place	Date	Title
Helsinki	1906-11-07	Uusmaalainen
Helsinki	1906-11-07	Helsingin Sanomat
Turku	1906-11-08	Uusi Aura
Helsinki	1906-11-08	Elämä
Tampere	1906-11-08	Tampereen Sanomat
Turku	1906-11-08	Sosialisti
Helsinki	1906-11-08	Uusi Suometar
Jyväskylä	1906-11-09	Suomalainen
Oulu	1906-11-09	Kaleva
Kuopio	1906-11-09	Pohjois-Savo
Tampere	1906-11-09	Kansan Lehti
Viipuri	1906-11-09	Karjala
Sortavala	1906-11-10	Laatokka
Heinola	1906-11-10	Heinolan Sanomat
Savonlinna	1906-11-10	Keski-Savo
Joensuu	1906-11-10	Karjalatar
Lahti	1906-11-11	Lahden Lehti
Kemi	1906-11-12	Pohjois-Suomi
Kristiina	1906-11-12	Etelä-Pohjanmaa
Lahti	1906-11-13	Lahti

Table 4: Reprints of a bank robbery news.

5 Conclusion

We have presented the use of the BLAST method to analyze text reuse in a massive corpus of historical newpapers of poor OCR quality. We have shown that, given sufficient computational power, the method is capable of identifying reprinted text passages that, due to OCR noise, may differ in up to 60% characters when aligned. Analysis of the clusters discovered by the method provides us with new insights into the magnitude and different types of text reuse, and reveals a number of individual examples of historical interest. As a future work, we will strive to develop a text classifier of the different types and topics of text reuse to be able to provide their quantitative analysis. The software developed to carry out the study will be made publicly available as open-source.

Acknowledgments

The work was supported by the research consortium *Computational History and the Transformation of Public Discourse in Finland, 1640-1910*, funded by the Academy of Finland. Computational resources were provided by CSC — IT Centre for Science, Espoo, Finland.

References

Stephen F. Altschul, Warren Gish, Webb Miller, Eugene W. Myers, and David J. Lipman. 1990. Basic local alignment search tool. *Journal of Molecular Biology*, 215(3):403–410, Oct.

Ryan Cordell. 2015. Reprinting, Circulation, and the Network Author in Antebellum Newspapers. *American Literary History*, 27(3):417–445.

Kimmo Kettunen. 2016. Keep, change or delete? setting up a low resource ocr post-correction framework for a digitized old finnish newspaper collection. In D. Calvanese, D. De Nart, and C. Tasso, editors, *Digital Libraries on the Move. IRCDL 2015. Communications in Computer and Information Science*, volume 612. Springer, Cham.

Tuula Pääkkönen, Jukka Kervinen, Asko Nivala, Kimmo Kettunen, and Eetu Mäkelä. 2016. Exporting Finnish Digitized Historical Newspaper Contents for Offline Use. *D-Lib Magazine*, 22(7).

David A. Smith, Ryan Cordell, Elizabeth Maddock Dillon, Nick Stramp, and John Wilkerson. 2014. Detecting and modeling local text reuse. In *Proceedings of the 14th ACM/IEEE-CS Joint Conference on Digital Libraries*, JCDL '14, pages 183–192, Piscataway, NJ, USA. IEEE Press.

David A. Smith, Ryan Cordell, and Abby Mullen. 2015. Computational Methods for Uncovering Reprinted Texts in Antebellum Newspapers. *American Literary History*, 27(3):E1–E15.

Aleksi Vesanto, Asko Nivala, Tapio Salakoski, Hannu Salmi, and Ginter Filip. 2017. A system for identifying and exploring text repetition in large historical document corpora. In *Proceedings of NoDaLiDa 2017*.

Association for Computational Linguistics
209 N. Eighth Street
Stroudsburg, Pennsylvania 18360

ISBN 978-1-5108-4336-3

9 781510 843363

CURRAN ASSOCIATES INC.
proceedings.com